¿CUÁNTAS PÍSCAS?

¿CUÁNTAS PÍSCAS?

A Latino's Lonely Journey To Success

NOÉ LARA

¿Cuántas Píscas?

Copyright © 2019 by Noé Lara. All rights reserved.

No part of this publication may be reproduced, stored in a retrieval system or transmitted in any way by any means, electronic, mechanical, photocopy, recording or otherwise without the prior permission of the author except as provided by USA copyright law.

The opinions expressed by the author are not necessarily those of URLink Print and Media.

1603 Capitol Ave., Suite 310 Cheyenne, Wyoming USA 82001
1-888-980-6523 | admin@urlinkpublishing.com

URLink Print and Media is committed to excellence in the publishing industry.

Book design copyright © 2019 by URLink Print and Media. All rights reserved.

Published in the United States of America

ISBN 978-1-64367-841-2 (Paperback)
ISBN 978-1-64367-840-5 (Digital)

Non-Fiction
12.09.19

ACKNOWLEDGEMENT

I wish to express my gratitude to my brothers and sisters who provided me their time and memories to support the facts in my story. I would also like to thank my wife Diana and our friends Lowell and Loretta Tollefson, and Sharon Neitzel for making sure that I expressed myself in the most professional way possible. Also, I am indebted to my friend Dr. Richard Melzer for his suggestions regarding story balance and structure.

    Finally, I want to express my gratitude to our Creator, who gave me the inspiration and confidence that enabled me to give this book life.

FOR

My father, el señor don Davíd Lara. You tried to warn me and show me the way, and *yo muy terco* (I stubbornly) at the time, did not listen.

CONTENTS

Acknowledgement 5
Preface 11
Introduction 13

Chapter 1:   Younger Years, 1950-1953 15
Chapter 2:   Travels to El Norte 26
Chapter 3:   The End of our Gypsy Migrant Life 31
Chapter 4:   Wall Controversy—I am just saying! 33
Chapter 5:   Beginning of a Formal Education 36
Chapter 6:   A Home of our Own 57
Chapter 7:   High School Years 62
Chapter 8:   Texas Tech Bound, 1964-1969 71
Chapter 9:   Dream Realized, 1969-2005 79
Chapter 10: End of a Challenging Career 105
Chapter 11: Mi Familia (My Family) 109
Chapter 12: Mis Hijos (My Children) 129
Chapter 13: My Second Marriage, 1995-present 133
Chapter 14: Spiritual Development 142
Chapter 15: Those That Made an Impact on My Life 151
Chapter 16: Lessons Learned 162
Chapter 17: How do you Spell Success? 168

About the Author 187

PREFACE

I was encouraged to write this book by friends and colleagues that would hear my story and personal thoughts and find them amusing and thought-provoking. I also wanted to revisit events in my life and the feelings that they evoked. Feelings that I still experience and that have helped shape my life.

Another goal was to honor my family, especially my Mexican-immigrant parents who struggled so hard with so little to ensure that I took advantage of the opportunities that presented themselves. Opportunities that could help me grow. My older brothers and sisters also sacrificed much to ensure that the youngest in the family of 12 would be better educated than they. This included my younger brother Danny, sister Connie, and me.

I included stories and shared experiences as a migrant and seasonal farmworker traveling to the state of Wisconsin and Lubbock Texas in search of work in the fields either picking vegetables or picking cotton. After completing college and after marriage, I also had an opportunity to work in the nation's capitol Washington D.C. and for the Housing Assistance Council (HAC), a national housing corporation dedicated to improving housing conditions in rural areas.

I proudly share my experiences in my adoptive state of New Mexico. My experiences in D.C. helped me prepare for the position of Executive Director of the HAC field office in Albuquerque. In 1980, I was recruited by New Mexico Governor Bruce King to head the New Mexico Housing Authority. After a brief stint in the private sector (Real Estate and Development), I pursued opportunities working as a social worker, social worker supervisor, and County Office Manager. For 20 years I also taught as an adjunct professor, at the University of New Mexico, Valencia Campus.

In the book I talk about the walls that often present challenges to immigrant young people as they pursue the American Dream. I describe the obstacles faced as immigrants adjust to a new culture and to a world that many times looks down on people that do not speak English and that don't share the same skin color. It will describe the author's struggle to obtain an education in a hostile environment marked by poverty, ignorance, and prejudiced attitudes. The author also gives an account of his disappointments with his struggles to achieve the "American Dream".

Religion is explored as it had a tremendous impact on the author- both positive and negative. Growing up in a Mexican-American protestant home was not an easy task as there was much guilt to go around. Yet it was this same faith that helped me steer in the right direction. The writer describes his new gained perspective as he reminisces about his past, enabling him to reflect on the reasons that he then acted the way he did, and how those actions and beliefs have influenced the way he lives his life today.

INTRODUCTION

I titled the book? *Cuantas Piscas? A Latino's Lonely Journey to Success.* "Cuántas píscas" means "How much do you pick?" This is referring to how much cotton someone is capable of picking. Just as young men had lines that they used when picking up a girl with a romantic intention, this line was used to begin a conversation with girls who were picking cotton in the same field. Of course, assertive girls were using the same line with the guys. To me the word has a double meaning. I interpret it to mean, what are you capable of accomplishing? or, what is your potential? To me it also begs the character question, what kind of a person are you?

I believe that it is important that we reflect from time to time, and evaluate the progress we are making in life's journey. Sometimes because we are prone to depression or because we are driven to depression, the road to success can be very lonely indeed. It's important to remember that many times we experience success only if we make changes. I believe that if we fail to accept change, we limit and sometimes deny ourselves any possibility of reaching our full potential. I discuss how I approached my journey, how others described my success and how I personally described my success.

My Mexican heritage, my spiritual upbringing, and my education, served as a beacon for my positive endeavors in my life. It was not easy for me to compete in an Anglo-dominated society. Because of this I had to work doubly hard to first obtain an education, and secondly, to be successful in some of my career choices. The faith that I inherited from my parents served to keep me from giving up, even though many times I was tempted to do so. My Christian background helped me to sustain a positive attitude toward challenges encountered and to be understanding toward those that did not wish for me to succeed.

My culture, my job experiences, and my faith contributed immensely to the path I chose in life, including some of the successes that I have had. I enjoyed a great deal of support from my older brothers and sisters and from some very special people who believed in me and who never gave up on me. But it was definitely my father and mothers' love and the stability they provided that had the greatest influence.

I hope that the reader will get a glimpse of my past, which many times was serious and hard, but also find some humor in my depiction of life back then.

CHAPTER 1

Younger Years, 1950-1953

There were thirteen children born to my parents, don David and doña Lola, as they were respectfully referred to by their friends. Because they were Christians and many of their friends were church families, they were also referred to as *Hermano y Hermana Lara* (Brother and Sister Lara). To my siblings and me, we respectfully called them Apá and Amá.

Twelve children survived into adulthood, seven sisters and five brothers. All of us were born approximately two years apart. I was the eleventh born, and I have two younger siblings, a brother Daniel (Danny) and a sister Consuelo (Connie).

When Connie was about five years old, my mother became pregnant with twins. Unfortunately, the pregnancy resulted in stillbirths. Had they lived, my mother would have given birth to fifteen children.

I was born at Kennedy Ranch in Williamson County, Texas. I was delivered by doña Petra, a midwife who delivered many of the babies on the ranch. I believe only three of my siblings were not delivered at home. I really do not remember living at Kennedy Ranch. However, a few years ago, my brother Estévan, who was nine years my senior and who retired to Elgin took me there and showed me the house where I was born. It is a small house surrounded by trees and situated near a livestock tank.

I have always celebrated my birthday on July 3rd and believed that I was born in 1945. In 2000, my wife and I were planning a trip to Europe. In the process of getting a passport, I had to produce a birth certificate. I did not have one, so I ordered one from Austin, where the archives are kept for those who were born in Texas. Upon receiving it, I was surprised that it indicated that I was born on September 3, 1944. I do not know when I was really born but I had to change my legal papers to reflect the September 3, 1944 date. I believe that my father, when registering my birth, just had too many things on his mind and probably was registering two or three births that day and could not quite remember the exact date when I was born. Several of my brothers and sisters also had similar problems establishing true birth dates. I have been getting a lot of mileage out of this, however, as I now celebrate two birthdays a year!

Apparently Kennedy Ranch was the home of many immigrants who came from Mexico looking for work. At one time it had its own school and grocery store. My older brothers have some very fond memories of the ranch, and it seems that my father and my older brothers were treated very well by Rankin Kennedy, the owner of the ranch.

Apá was born in San Rafael, Nuevo Leon, Méjico. This is a community south of Nuevo Laredo and north of Monterrey, Mexico. I always thought that Amá was born in Mexico, but I learned later in life that she was actually born in a rural Texas town called Big Foot. Proof of her birth could not be established because the court house of that county had burned. She was in her fifties before she was able to get a birth certificate.

She did this by finding two witnesses who could attest to her birth. It was important for her to prove that she was an American citizen. Prior to this my mother was always reluctant to go to Mexico for fear that the authorities would not allow her to return to the United States.

My earliest recollection of living anywhere was in a small town called Thrall in Williamson County, Texas. It actually was not too far from Kennedy Ranch and some 20 miles from Austin, the State Capitol. We lived in a little compound of three houses. The road leading to our house ended when it got to our houses. We lived with Apá and Amá in the largest of the three houses. At this time, there were ten of us living with our parents. My brother Paul, his wife Lourdes, and their son Augustine lived across the street in a smaller house. There was a third house next to Paul's house that was designated to be my brother David's when he got married. In the meanwhile, it was always rented to someone else.

Every year, after following the crops, we would return to Thrall and stay in our old house. When we stopped following the crops to the Midwest and settled in Lubbock, we would still occasionally visit the old house. It wasn't until years later that my father sold the property to his brother, my *tío* (uncle) Enrique.

Our house in Thrall was very cold in winter and hot in the summer. It had no insulation and was heated by firewood and coal. It had no plumbing, and we got our water from a man-made well. A pail was attached to a rope that we would lower to retrieve water for our use. We would transfer that water to another pail that we would take in the house. This pail was called a *tina* and we called the tin dipper with the long extension a *dipa*. Getting water from the well was one of the jobs of the kids, so I did my share. Every time that we returned to live in the house, my brother Paul, who was small in stature, would be hoisted down the well to remove any debris that had collected so that the water would be suitable to drink.

The restrooms were outhouses located about 75 yards from the house. Walking to them in the cold of winter presented a different challenge. The distance and the bitter cold winds made it exceedingly unpleasant to perform basic bodily functions. In the summer while using the outhouse, which we called *el escusado,* we were constantly vigilant for snakes, spiders, and other critters that might bite us!

Kennedy Ranch House

Written by Noé Lara
February 15, 2007

I was born in a ranch house,
My family shared with me.
I don't remember living there,
But it's a place I'd like to be.

I was delivered by a midwife,
dona Petra was her name.
She made sure I cried my first,
Before she went away.

Cows were eating just nearby,
on this hot and dusty day.
Kids were waiting for my arrival,
to hurry up and play.

My mother was in labor,
My father standing by.
You could hear a pin drop,
when I refused to cry.

But after prayers and panic,
From my lungs erupted sound.
Everyone was relieved to know,
That I finally came around.

¿CUÁNTAS PÍSCAS?

This house where many others lived,
this home of love and pain.
Was shelter to my family,
Protection from the rain.

It now stands much in disrepair,
Since everyone has gone.
We still go by and visit,
Although no longer home.

I was born a little timid,
In this humble and peaceful ranch.
I know that through my family,
I've learned to take a chance.

They say our spirits still abide,
In this lone and dusty place.
They still hear children play,
and Amá singing Amazing Grace.

The house had a small picket fence in the front, and rose bushes were planted to the right of the house. It had one pear tree that my mother loved which was located near the well. She loved the fruit of the pear tree but she also liked the beautiful blossoms that the tree had in the Spring. In the back near the well was a washing house that my uncle Manuel, from Mexico, had built. It was a *cuartito*, a place where the laundry would be washed, and it was also a small storage area. There was always a big patch of cactus. Cactus provided food for us in the spring. We called this delicacy *nopalitos*, which everyone in the family enjoys to this day.

The kitchen was small and the cooking was done on a wood-burning stove that also served to partially heat the house in the winter. There was another wood stove in another room. I remember Apá placing little embers in our shoes so that they would be warm before we put them on as we would then walk about two miles to school. The winters were very cold in East Texas.

Our little white *casita* (house) was surrounded by cotton fields owned by a man named Mr. Stiles. Sometimes we could see men plowing the fields, using mules to pull the plows. I could time when my father would be coming home from work by observing when these men started taking the plows off the mules and began leading them home. Once they did this, I knew that my father would soon be home. Although we no longer lived there, Apa would also still work at the Kennedy ranch from time to time.

At that time we did not have refrigerators or iceboxes, so meals were pretty simple and we ate foods that did not require refrigeration. Mainly our diet consisted of beans, rice, potatoes, and tortillas. Sometimes on special occasions or on weekends we had a little meat. Apá would use a term that sounded funny, but I can now see its practicality. He said that the tortillas were used to *"engañar la gorda."* What he meant was that there wasn't enough of the meat on the plate, so we should eat a little bit at a time and, if you eat a lot of tortillas, it would make it seem as if we ate a lot of meat. In essence, we would fool our stomachs into thinking they'd gotten a lot of meat!

Sometimes in the summer a man would come around in his truck selling ice. We were happy when my mother bought a block of ice. The kids would be given a small piece each to cool them down. My mother would also make us some *pinole* as a special treat. Pinole is toasted corn, ground up with sugar. She would make little cones out of paper, fill them with pinole and hand them out to us.

One Sunday my mother endeavored to make a special meal called *mole*. This was chicken with special corn gravy that included chocolate and other ingredients. I really liked this and that Sunday, I ate three bowls of it. I guess I ate too much as I became deathly ill, throwing up every bit of what I had eaten. To this day, I cannot stand even the smell of mole!

Three of my older sisters and I attended school in Thrall. I was about six years old at the time. The older siblings had already dropped out of school, and my younger brother Danny was too young for school. We walked to school even though it was quite far. I guess there was no bus transportation at the time, because I remember seeing many other kids also walking.

I did not enjoy school very much at the time. I was very shy and knew very little English. I was very conscious that I could not speak English, and there were no bilingual teachers. Most of the time, our being in school was a waste of time, as we understood very little of what was going on and there did not seem to be a genuine interest on the school's part to help us learn.

I do not remember having close friends in school other than family members. At least, I didn't have friends that I would play with after school. Sometimes at home we played with some of the African-American kids who lived nearby. For some reason, I do not remember that we were ever encouraged to seek them out for playmates. I do remember that one little girl, Maybelene, used to come over and play with my sister Elizabeth.

We took a lunch to school which consisted of a tortilla cut in a square and some *jalea* (jam). The tortilla was cut in a square to resemble white bread because the Anglo kids would make fun of our eating tortillas.

Walking home, Catholic nuns would drive down the street encouraging kids to go to catechism. We did not as we were attending a Mexican Presbyterian church in nearby Taylor.

I got little encouragement to succeed from teachers, although I do recall one incident. As the teacher took us out to see the Boy Scouts put up the flag, a teacher told me that if I learned English, I would someday also be allowed to put up the flag.

As we were walking home one day, a Coca Cola truck stopped, and the driver gave me three red pencils with the Coca Cola logo. I thought this was a very nice gesture and, whenever I would see a Coca Cola truck after that, it made me feel good inside. I remember one time that the school took us on a picnic in a park in nearby Taylor. I had never been to a picnic before so didn't know what to expect. In fact, my parents were surprised that they had taken me to a picnic, as they did not remember having been notified. I did not take a picnic lunch, so the teacher made me a plate from whatever other people brought. This was the first time that I tasted a wonderful delicacy called potato salad.

I spent a lot of time playing with my nephew Augustine (Augie) who is one year younger than me. Even though he is a nephew, he is also older than my younger brother and sister. It seemed that whatever toy he got, I always got one similar to his. We enjoyed his mother Lourdes reading to us from comic books. I did not learn until later that she did not know how to read. She was a wonderful story teller, and it didn't make any difference to us if the stories were not accurate. For that matter, the stories she told us might have been more interesting than the way they were actually written!

For something to do, we would often hunt for pop bottles and, when we had enough, trade them for pop and candy. We traded the bottles at a gas station nearby called Laymon's. Mr. Laymon was a chubby man who was always smoking a cigar. One year Augie and I both got tricycles. We would race down the road on them shouting, "*El cachetón del puro!*" I think it was an attempt to make fun of Mr. Laymon. At the same time, however, we repeated those words because we thought they sounded so funny! The words mean "the chubby cheek man with a cigar."

¿CUÁNTAS PÍSCAS?

As a kid, I was somewhat adventuresome. I got it in my head to hitchhike to Taylor, several miles away. I was seven years old at the time. My brother David, who is eleven years my senior, told me that it was not a good idea because there was a possibility that no one would pick me up. Secondly, it was possible that, if they did, the person would expect that I would give him some money. Since I had none, I decided not to risk it. There was no mention of safety factors, as in those days people felt very safe hitchhiking.

Even though we owned our own home, we were still very poor. One day I found an egg in our yard. I wanted to have my mother cook it for me. However, my mother said that it did not belong to us. It was from a neighbor's hen that had wandered into our yard, so it was the neighbor's egg. She made me take it back to her. I was hoping that the neighbor would give it to me, but she didn't. I believe that they were just as poor as we were.

It was always pleasant when we got new shoes. Until I was about fourteen, I always slept on the floor. When I got shoes, I would place them near my pallet, as they would smell so good when I got up in the morning. Getting new shoes was a big deal for us. One time, my brother Paul was driving us home from Taylor. Since I had gotten new shoes, he said I didn't need the old ones so he threw them out the window. I remember feeling sorry for my old shoes and really wanting them back. Of course, he was joking, and he turned the vehicle around and got them for me. I still feel the same way with old cars I have traded or clothes that I have had for a long time. It is really hard for me to get rid of old things, as I easily grow attached. It's one of the problems with being poor.

My father would go to Mexico to visit his father and brothers and sisters frequently when I was very young, and we were living in Thrall. He would travel by train. I remember hearing the train whistle at night and my believing that Apá would be coming home on that train. Apá would always bring souvenirs, Mexican candy, and *pan dulce* (pastries). I am sure this is the reason that to this day I still enjoy trains and songs about trains.

Sometimes we would be visited by relatives from Mexico. My uncles usually came to work but, on occasion, an aunt would come just to visit. This was my father's younger sister, Consuelo (Chelo), who was about the same age as my older sisters. She was very pretty and had a wonderful sense of humor. She was a good story teller and taught us many songs in Spanish. The youngest girl of the family, Connie was named after this aunt. Mi *tía* (aunt) Chelo now lives in Berkeley, California and enjoys her many grandchildren, who are Black, Oriental, and Anglo. She says that her house often resembles the United Nations.

Apá was always known for being very resourceful, as he always seemed to be hustling jobs to generate money to feed our large family. It was not unusual for Apá to take his big truck and several men to the woods and cut cedar trees to make posts to sell. They would camp out all week, and when they came home they would bring a truck full of wood to sell or for our use. Sometimes they would bring a rabbit or two that they had killed. If we were lucky, they would also bring us some pecans. Pecans grow wild by the rivers in east Texas. This was a big treat for all of us, so we looked forward to the men coming home.

Apá made it a point to talk to me about el *Diez y Seis de Septiembre,* the sixteenth of September, which is Mexican Independence Day. In the community where we lived, there were still many who were recent arrivals from Mexico and still held on to their patriotism, including my father. They would celebrate *el Diez y Seis* for a whole week with dances, games, and, of course, lots of food and music.

I remember Apá taking me to a celebration where we heard speeches by older men gifted in speech-making. One speech was referred to as "*El Grito.*" This was to commemorate when Padre Miguel Hidalgo issued the call for independence from Spain in 1810. This was formally called "*El Grito de la Independencia,*" "the Call for Independence". I could see the passion of patriotism in the eyes of these men when they gave their speeches. I also would see a little moisture in Apá's eyes as he listened attentively. To this day, even though I was born in this country, I myself get goose bumps when I hear the Mexican National Anthem.

For many years Apá would only listen to a radio tuned to Mexican stations. Whenever he got a chance, he would buy a

Mexican newspaper called *La Prensa*. He always wanted to find out what was going on in Mexico, where all of his brothers and sisters still lived. Apá never did become an American citizen, although he had opportunities. Somehow he got the idea that if he became an American citizen he would be forced to step on the Mexican flag. This he was unwilling to do. We would tell him that this wasn't the case, but he did not want to take a chance. He did live in this country legally, having been issued a green card which enabled him to work.

During my earlier years, at home everyone spoke Spanish, most of our friends were Latino, and we attended a Spanish-speaking church. Moreover, we listened to Spanish music, and Amá cooked and we ate Mexican food. All of us were encouraged to learn to read and write in Spanish. The Mexican culture was very strong as I was growing up!

CHAPTER 2

Travels to El Norte

El Norte was what we called the states in the North or Midwest that many Mexican-American families traveled to while in the migrant stream. First, we went with *mi tío* (my uncle) Magdaleno. He was married to my mother's sister, *mi tía* Elena. Later Apá bought his own big truck, and we were able to go on our own. My family traveled to *El Norte* to follow the crops for approximately ten years.

I have fond memories of our experiences while in the migrant stream. In Thrall, I remember my mother commenting to my older sisters as she looked out the window and saw big trucks with tarps on top driving down the highway, "there go the Flores" or some other family they knew that appeared to be going north. The beds of large trucks were modified by attaching wooden arches and these were covered with a tarp so that families could ride in the back protected from the elements as they made the long trip north. Also, my family would usually listen to a Spanish radio stations, often announced that such and such family got its truck blessed, preparing to go to El Norte. This meant that we would be going, too.

From East Texas, we traveled to the state of Wisconsin. We first went to Brillion, a rural town where sugar beet crops were abundant. Then we would travel to Sturgeon Bay to pick cherries. Our last stop was in Ocanto, where we would pick cucumbers that would eventually be pickled and bottled. I still remember the smell of vinegar as I rode in the back of Apá's truck on trips into town.

Sometimes we went to Brillion first, for the sugar beet thinning, and then returned later to help harvest the sugar beet crop. Workers used a long machete with a hook in front to pick up the beets and then chop the greens from them. When the weather was bad, or if we happened to arrive a little early, some of the men would go to work in the English pea factories.

It was always a surprise to see which houses would be assigned to each family. Sometimes several families lived in one house, if the house was a big one. Some were large dilapidated brick homes. You could tell that long ago they were mansions occupied by very rich people. One place in particular had a very large basement and an attic. Rumors of ghosts inhabiting the houses were common. While exploring the attic in one house, my sister Ester found a prosthetic leg. Everyone swore that at night that leg could be heard walking up and down the stairs. Also, there was an old piano. People would report that at night they could hear someone playing it. Superstition ran rampant among our group.

My father would use his vehicles to take families from south Texas to Wisconsin, some 1,200 miles away. He was also responsible for making sure that they got to work and for negotiating contracts for them to work in the fields. Many of the families were related to us, but some were just friends or acquaintances of friends.

One trip, Apá fell asleep at the wheel, and we went off the road, plunging into a large ditch. It frightened us, and the ordeal of getting the old '46 Plymouth out was horrendous. The car had landed on a steep incline and, had the car not stopped, Apá and his passengers would have been killed. This of course included me. Eventually a wrecker came and pulled us out, allowing us to proceed to our destination.

I will always remember the times we stopped on the side of the road to sleep. At night I could hear the large semi trucks making these very interesting sounds. At first you could barely hear them. As they got nearer, the roar of the trucks would increase and, as they passed by, the sound would again decrease. It sounded as if a swarm of bees were moving toward and then away from us.

At least once a year Christian missionaries would visit the migrant camps. They would bring us Bibles and show us movies about the Bible. Sometimes they would have some gifts to give for the children. There were many who enjoyed this attention.

One day, our men saw an Anglo family butchering a steer. They approached these men and politely asked for the cow's stomach to make *menudo*, a delicacy among Mexican–Americans. The next day, several Anglo families brought over several sacks of groceries. I guess they thought that we must be starving to death, as we had requested that they give us the entrails of a cow, parts that they normally threw away.

My father always considered the children of the camp. Once a year he would take his big truck, and he would take all of the kids to the movies. This was a big treat for all of us. Children were important because field work was an opportunity for large families to make money, as children of any age could work. I remember picking cherries and my father telling me that once I picked four buckets of cherries I didn't have to work anymore. It seemed, however, that I would eat just about as many cherries as I picked!

Other fond memories were of when we would go to the landfills. We always found toys, and we had a wonderful time looking for treasures. The same thing happened when we would first arrive at labor camps. We would always explore the property looking for things that other people had left behind. We developed a signal to indicate who would possess a treasure if two kids had spotted it at the same time. We would say, *"Banjo Zero"*. If we did not say it in time and another person said it, even though we might have picked the item up, it belonged to that kid. You had to be quick in claiming your treasure!

I had my first taste of beer in Wisconsin when I was about eight years old. Some of the men in the camp would go drinking during the weekend. On Monday mornings, the women would get all the left-over beer and got rid of it by throwing the bottles in the outhouses. One day, some of the older kids fished the bottles out and cleaned them up a bit. We then went to the bushes and proceeded to drink the beer. I remember the taste, as I was coerced to drink by the older kids. It tasted horrible, especially because I knew that just a few minutes before it had been in a pit of feces. I don't remember having a desire to drink beer again for many years, or until I went to college.

There was always something to do as migrant farm workers. One of the activities was listening to don Domingo tell stories. Don Domingo was my brother Paul's father-in-law. He was a very good storyteller and would entertain young and old alike with his stories told around the fire. An old favorite was a story about *La Llorona* (The Weeper). There are many versions of this story that are told throughout this country and in Mexico. However, the theme is pretty much the same.

According to the legend, a beautiful young woman marries a man, and she has several children with him. He stays away most of the time, and finally he leaves for good. To be free to find another husband, and because she doesn't have money to feed her children, she takes them to the river and drowns them. When she came to her senses, she was remorseful and went back to the river, crying uncontrollably for what she had done. She killed herself and afterwards was condemned for all eternity to wander by the river, wailing as she looks for her children. She usually comes out when there is a full moon.

When I was a kid, this story was also told to keep us in line. Adults would tell us that if we didn't behave, the *Qu Qui* (boogyman), or la *Llorona*, would get us.

Don Domingo's stories were always scary but each had a moral. Another story was about a young woman who loved to go to dances. She would party with many men, even though her mother would always counsel her to stay home and be a good girl. One day she went to a dance against her mother's will. She met up with a very handsome man who charmed her into falling in love with him. She was having a great time until the end of the dance, when she happened to look down at his feet. She was shocked to find that one foot was a rooster's leg and the other was a horse's hoof. Also, those attending the dance were overcome with a stench of sulfur. Everyone came to the conclusion that he was Lucifer himself, so they all started running home. After that, according to his story, she always listened to her mother and became a decent girl.

I love to listen to and sing country western music. The songs I like to sing, however, are the sad old Hank Williams ballads. I was introduced to his music when I was very young, while working in the fields in Wisconsin. My brothers would put the radio on when they got to the car, which was located at the end of the crop rows. A song that was very popular then, and which has become one of my favorites, was *Jambalaya*.

Overall, our trips to El Norte were productive and interesting. They were productive because Apá would make pretty good money, and they were interesting because we got to see another part of the country. I really liked the Anglo people in Wisconsin. They did not harbor the prejudices that many Anglos in Texas did at the time. They also showed many acts of kindness, such as the groceries that they brought over or the visits by the missionaries. The farmers whose crops we picked always provided a party for the workers after the crop-picking season was over. We all looked forward to these parties, where they dispensed lots of food, drinks, and chocolate candy bars.

After harvesting the crops in El Norte, we would travel to West Texas to pick cotton. The last time that we traveled to West Texas, our destination was Lubbock. I remember my mother getting a letter from my sister Marta who, with her husband and new-born baby, lived in Lubbock at the time. An arrangement had been made that we would live on the farm where they lived, and we would pick cotton for their landlord. At the bottom of the letter to my mother, Marta drew a little puppy with a turned up tail. She said that it was waiting for me, as it would belong to me. I was very excited to leave for Texas to meet my new dog!

CHAPTER 3

The End of our Gypsy Migrant Life

After we arrived in Lubbock, Texas, and toward the end of the cotton picking season, my brother Paul was offered a full-time job at the Buddy and Royce Turnbow farm nearby. He was Apá's truck driver, so we decided to also stay in Lubbock. Also, Amá had not been feeling very well, and it made sense that we step out of the migrant stream for one year. As it turned out, we never returned to Wisconsin following the crops. Instead, we became seasonal farm workers in Lubbock County.

My brother Estévan also got a job with the Turnbows, while my brother David and my father got jobs with S.O. Adamson at a nearby farm. We lived on the Adamson farm for several years. S.O. Adamson provided housing and, as substandard as it was, we had a place to stay rent-free. First we moved to a *campito*, a row of tiny living units that accommodated seasonal farm workers such as ourselves. The units were constructed out of concrete blocks and had no plumbing. The units were not insulated and sometimes you could see the outside through the bricks. They were heated by little coal stoves, and cooking was done on small butane burners. The water source and outhouses were a good distance away.

The family was separated because the rooms were so tiny. Still, we lived in units adjacent to each other. It was not possible to bathe daily, so we would wash our faces really well in the morning in a pan that we called *lavamanos*. When we bathed, we used a number three tub that we would bring in the house. The number three tub was the largest laundry tubs made; it was round and was aluminum. We would heat some water on the stove and fill the tub. Usually we bathed on Saturdays, taking turns to insure privacy. We bathed at least once a week. Eventually we moved to a little house on the same farm, where we lived for a few more years until we were able to buy a house of our own.

The little house that we moved into had two bedrooms and a large kitchen. My older brothers slept in the nicest of the bedrooms, and my sisters, Danny, and I slept in the other one. My parents slept in part of the kitchen. By this time, two of my older sisters, Marta and Chila, and my brother, Paul, were already married. Therefore, there were ten people living in this little house, including Apá and Amá.

The house was not very well insulated and had no indoor plumbing. Both the water source and the toilets were several yards away from the house, and we had no refrigeration. The heating source was butane, so we had one small heater in my brothers' bedroom and another in the kitchen. The bedroom where Danny, my sisters, and I slept was mainly used for sleeping, as there was not much room to do anything else. My older brothers' room was a little nicer and roomier, so we would use it as a *sala*, or room to entertain visitors. Danny and I slept on pallets on the floor. I do not remember a time when we did not share our pallets with bedbugs. It seemed that no matter what we did, we could not get rid of them. I often prayed for daybreak so I would not have to endure being bitten by these little stinky blood-sucking critters.

The outside of the house was stucco. However, it had no finish to it and was a discolored light grey color. The house had a row of trees on the north side which provided shade for our cars in the summer. To the east was a highway, and the sound of traffic could be heard at all hours. It was a farm that had ample space to play, and it was here that I learned to ride a bike and play baseball.

CHAPTER 4

Wall Controversy—I am just saying!

My father don David Lara walked to Texas USA in 1919. He was 18 years old when he migrated from his home town of San Rafael, Nuevo Leon Méjico. There are many families that back then and now, continue to immigrate to the US to escape poverty, wars, or home grown terrorists such as gangs.

At the time that my father crossed the border, separation from the two countries, Mexico and the US, was no more than a line in the sand or a walk or swim over a shallow Rio Grande River.

No one talked about *Walls* and the people coming across, for the most part, were welcomed as their labor contributed to the success of many American farmers and the construction and food industries. As a matter of fact to help farmers harvest crops such as cotton, a program was developed. Contracts for workers were developed between the United States and Mexico enabling many to enter legally into the country under the Bracero Program. Mexican immigrants would pick the crops and return to Mexico at the end of the season. The end of this program resulted in returning to import labor from Mexico illegally. Although they came to this country illegally, not much was done to discourage their coming, as their participation was essential to the agriculture, food, and construction industries. Many also worked in homes of well-to-do families as maids or gardeners.

During times of war, Mexican immigrants again proved valuable because they harvested the crops that would feed the soldiers. As well, many volunteered to serve in the military putting their own lives on the line. From a political point of view, there was not much in the a way of laws or policies as many immigrants were valued for their contributions. Before 1980, there were no laws about hiring unauthorized immigrants. It wasn't until *The Reform and Control Act of 1986* that employers had limits on who they could hire.

Situations have changed somewhat since my father came over to look for work and to start a family. Presently, there doesn't a day go by that we don't hear from those that believe that a *Wall* is needed to keep immigrants out fearing that they will take over much needed jobs or bring in illegal drugs or unsavory characters that will contribute to crime. The topic of immigration and a *Wall* generates much tension and animosity among the politicians and the human rights sector.

Society has changed quite a bit since those innocent days when my father crossed the border. There now exists a growing American appetite to consume illegal drugs. As long as there is a market, drug-producing countries like Mexico, will continue to supply the market demand. However, what the *Wall* advocates fail to see is that these suppliers are a lot more sophisticated and deal in volumes. They own their own planes and many have dug tunnels to transfer the drugs. We know that most of the drugs that come into the country come through established ports of entry and not through isolated areas in the desert, negating the need for a wall stretching from Texas to California. The federal government reports tell us that most drugs and illegal crossers come through official ports of entry, hidden in vehicle compartments or carried by a crosser and not in unguarded areas that currently don't have a wall. I acknowledge that *walls* are needed on the border to secure the legal crossing of people from one country to another. *Walls* have always been needed and used near ports of entry and in urban areas.

Historically *walls* have been built in other countries and in different times. The French, the British, the Germans, and of course the Chinese with their Great Wall of China. All have eventually been abandoned.

The Department of Homeland Security estimates that the proposed wall would cost $22 Billion dollars. This Wall would extend from Texas, through New Mexico and Arizona, to California. This cost does not include maintenance or property acquisition. Many experts also propose that the construction of the *wall* would do little to deter crime or stop those that risk their own lives for an opportunity to flee the atrocities and famine that they witness every day and in their country.

More recently, immigrants from Guatemala, Honduras, and El Salvador are traveling hundreds of miles in caravans to cross the US border. Their goal, however, is to cross the border and seek asylum. They want to get caught! Again, they are bringing their families which many times also come with health issues. For health, economic and social reasons, we in the US, have to overhaul the entire immigration system and it must be done in a realistic and nonpolitical manner.

CHAPTER 5

Beginning of a Formal Education

Lubbock County was where my younger brother Danny, my sister Connie, and I got our education. For the first time we were able to stay in a location long enough to take advantage of a school system. My sister Elisabeth, who is two years older than me, also attended Frenship School. She agrees with me that, prior to attending school in Lubbock County, we were never taught much at the other schools. She talks about the joy she felt when she learned how to read. She compares it to not having good eyesight and suddenly getting glasses enabling her to see for the first time. She soon became an avid reader.

Elisabeth dropped out of school after completing the eighth grade so she could join the rest of the family in the fields. I always wondered what she could have become had she continued in school, as she is very intelligent and made very good grades. In those days, our parents had no expectation for any of us to get an education, much less girls.

I began going to a migrant program in the Frenship School District in a West Texas town called Wolfforth. The migrant program that I attended was not challenging, and I quickly got bored. In those days the West Texas school systems did not expect Hispanics to succeed in school. They especially did not expect migrants to complete an education. I believe that the migrant classes were set up simply because it was the law.

Later, I was transferred to regular classes, and I really began enjoying school. I loved school and strived for perfect attendance. One year in elementary school, I received a certificate for not missing a single day of school. Also, my father did not believe in people wasting time. If you chose not go to school, you had to work. You had to practically be on your death bed to stay at home doing nothing.

One day, as a teenager, and after we had moved into our own house, I felt sick with cold symptoms. I asked Apá if I could stay at home for the day. He agreed, but little did I know what he had in mind! He had me help him build a fence around a lake that was on the property. I really felt sick all day long. The next day, although not yet fully recovered, I went back to school. I can, however, proudly say that the fence is still standing today.

School was especially challenging for us younger kids as neither one of our parents could read or write English, and our older siblings had dropped out of school themselves at a very early age. There really was no one to help us with homework, and we had no reference books of any kind at home. I remember signing Apá's name on my report cards when they were sent home.

It was noisy in our house most of the time, making it nearly impossible to study. Many times, I would study in an old parked 1941 Chrysler that my brother David used to drive when he was younger and the car was operable. Given that no one in our family had any significant education, it wasn't surprising that there was not much push for us to continue our education.

We lived quite a few miles from the school and we relied on school bus transportation. One day, our bus was very late. Apparently it did not start up that morning. There was an Anglo girl who lived across the street who usually rode the bus with us. A new bus that went by the house to pick up other kids saw us standing waiting for our bus. The bus driver stopped and picked up the Anglo girl, but left us there. I will never forget this, as I saw that there were plenty of empty seats on the bus. That was the way of the world in those times.

In the fourth grade, my class went on a trip to a Lubbock television station so we could appear in a children's program, the Jack Huddle Show. All the kids were interviewed and asked whether they wanted to sing a song. I sang *Home on the Range*. The bad part about it was that my family did not have a T.V., so no one that was significant to me was able to view the show!

When I graduated from the eighth grade, I remember Apá talking to me about my getting a job with a farmer so I could begin earning my keep. A farmer would usually provide a small weekly salary and then allow a worker to harvest from seven to ten acres of cotton for himself, as a bonus. If the crop was good, the worker might make a little money at the end of the year. If not, it was just tough luck. Luckily, my father's boss had heard that I was making very good grades in school, and he shared this with my father, planting the thought that perhaps he should allow me to stay in school. My father respected Mr. Adamson, and I was allowed to continue in school.

I loved school, but I was always very shy. I never was the type of kid that got into trouble and, although I did very well, I was not one to volunteer any answers unless called upon by teachers. Despite this, I never had any trouble complying with what was required to make good grades.

Growing up, challenges came to me in three forms. Firstly, I struggled to fit into an Anglo-dominated world. Secondly, I was influenced by my parents to respect the old Mexican traditions and values. Thirdly, I was often confused by my parents' strict moral standards. They certainly didn't jive with the raging hormonal influences and the desire to be accepted by my peers, many of whom had parents who were more flexible.

I would often compare my father to my student friends' fathers in this farming community. My father always came up short because he did not own the land that we farmed, couldn't speak English, and was merely a laborer. Also, he was not educated and I perceived him to be superstitious. While irrigating, he would tell me many stories about our relatives in Mexico. Some I found hard to believe. For example, he would tell me that some people could change into animals such as a *lechusa* (burrowing owl). Others could actually break a glass by just looking at it with great concentration. I thought this to be pure superstition, but I listened respectfully just the same.

When I eventually went to college, a psychology professor had the class subscribe to *Psychology Today*, a magazine that printed studies describing a similar power. One day, an article came out which showed a Mexican man playing chess with someone while lying on his back in a dark room adjacent to his opponent's room. He would concentrate hard and visualize the board that he played on. Also, the magazine cited examples of people that could concentrate and be able to stop a clock or break a glass of water.

In cultural anthropology courses, I learned that Native American tribes share many of these same beliefs about men changing into birds. They call it shape-shifting. I also read Carlos Casteñeda's book, *The Teachings of Don Juan*. In the book, a shaman named don Juan teaches Carlos Castaneda how to change from a man into a bird. I began to realize that perhaps Apá wasn't all that off when he described what he heard or saw regarding the subjects of shape-shifting or other powers attributed to special people.

One winter day, as I was walking back from my brother Paul's house to our house, a distance of about three miles, I encountered a great owl. I was about 12 years old at the time. He was near our house and sitting on a post by the railroad tracks. I shot him in the stomach with my BB gun with the intention of scaring him and causing him to fly away. He was sitting on a fence pole that was directly in front of my path. I shot him three times, but he didn't even twitch.

Then I remembered what Apá had said about people changing into owls. I concluded that this was not an ordinary owl, but some bad person that had changed and who intended to do me harm. I ran as fast as I could, which was not very fast because there was pretty thick snow on the ground. I didn't look back for a while, but when I did, I did not see him following me. While I was running, I kept repeating, *"El nombre sea de Diosito"* (In the name of God). Amá taught us to use this little prayer when we encountered danger, among other things!

Apá also trained us to look at the cranes in the skies as it approached winter. If their flight patterns spelled an F, it meant that we were going to have a hard winter. Cold in Spanish is *Frío*. I never questioned how the cranes knew how to spell in Spanish.

Later in life, as an adult, I began to see Apá in a different light. Although he had challenges, he was a business man, a good father, and he taught us about God and a moral way of life. He always took us to church, and he never failed to put food on the table, even though times were bad.

He was also very considerate. There were many of us, but he never failed to bring home a case of Cokes and a cake for each of our birthdays. When my younger brother and I were old enough, he bought us bicycles. They were not new, but they were very nice. He knew that this meant a lot to us. He did not outwardly encourage us to play in sports, but he supported us once we made the decision to participate. Neither one of my parents was very vocal, but each was blessed with a great deal of faith, a good sense of humor, and a deep love for family.

On the Adamson farm we lived next door to a very nice Anglo family that had three children, their ages ranging from three to eight years of age. The dad, Cecil Vaughn, was a medic in the Air Force. We became very good friends and, as a result, Elisabeth, Danny, and I were invited to picnics and other outings with the family. My sister Elisabeth baby-sat for them on many occasions.

The Vaughn family took us fishing at a nearby lake. It was the first time that we had gone to a lake just to have fun. Also, Cecil took me rabbit hunting when he took his son Jarvis. We had a lot of fun, and my mother was pleased when I had brought home several cottontails for dinner.

Dale Vaughn was the middle son. He was about six years old and was a good-looking kid with a lot of energy and a wonderful personality. One summer, we began to notice that he was not as active as he had always been. I was about ten years old at the time. We learned that he had been diagnosed with leukemia. Slowly, he deteriorated and eventually died. This was the first time that I had experienced the death of a child who was close to our family. His mother went into depression and eventually had to be hospitalized. We all took his death pretty hard.

I was about twelve when I embarked on my first money-making venture. I decided to raise frogs. Someone had told me that people would buy frogs to eat and that they were considered a delicacy. One day it rained a lot, and tadpoles were everywhere. I thought that this was my chance to go into business. We had a wash tub that had table legs. I filled it with water and proceeded to catch tadpoles and put them in the tub. I would feed them and change the water regularly, and, to me, it appeared that they were thriving. One day I came home from school and found all of them gone. At first I could not figure out what had happened, but soon I found the problem. They had lost their tails, grown legs, and simply hopped out of the tub! Later I found out that the frogs I was raising were not the edible kind anyway.

One year, Apá decided to raise some chickens. Some would provide us with eggs and others we would use for food, or so he thought. They came in the mail in large cartons with little holes on top. We had plenty of room as we now lived in a place with coops and barns. I soon learned that these little animals were carnivorous. When a baby chick fell and got hurt, the rest would proceed to peck it until it died. Afterwards, they would eat the chick a peck at a time. Many times, little chicks would drop to the ground as if they were dead. Apá would pick them up, put a coffee can over them, and bang on the can with a stick. This often caused the chicks to wake up. He would separate them until they got well and before the others pecked them to death.

When I was 16 and shortly before I went to work at Reese Air Force Base I worked for Mr. James, a farmer who looked very much like the actor Walter Brennen. At that time, a television program with Walter Brennen, called the "Real McCoys", was very popular. In fact, Mr. James talked like him, and he wore a big straw hat and overalls just like those worn by Walter Brennen on the show. The character, Grandpa McCoy, had a Mexican-American employee whose name was *Pepino* (cucumber). Just to be mean, my brothers and sisters started calling me Pepino.

Mr. James had a big field where he grew some delicious sweet corn. One day, he told me that I could take some green corn home for my family. He said to take as much as I wanted. The field was about a half mile from the road, so after he left for lunch I took a sack and proceeded to pick some corn to take home. I got a little carried away, as I filled the sack to the top. When I started home with it, I discovered that it weighed too much, and I couldn't carry it. I felt very guilty for taking so much of it, and I was afraid that Mr. James might get mad. So I dug a hole, buried enough to lighten the load, and took the rest of the corn home.

I enjoyed working for Mr. James because he was so funny. He was from somewhere in Appalachia and often had dozens of funny stories to share. It was a pleasure working for him.

Being poor and always living in remote rural areas far from the school contributed to my not participating in school events that could have provided me with much better social skills. I did play in Little League, as a neighbor friend's dad took us to the game and to some practice sessions. Sometimes, because I worked in the fields all day, I took my baseball uniform with me. I would wash up a little, and someone would pick me up from the fields to go directly to the game, as I was the pitcher. I would change into my uniform in the car. All of the Anglo kids would have these bright white uniforms, and you could see that they were well rested and smelled very clean. I was tired and somewhat dirty, but ready to play. In the game, I forgot about how I looked and how tired I was. I was thought to be a very good player.

I had a good friend named Billy Woodall who lived across the street from me. We would play together all of the time. We had a peculiar whistle that we used when we wanted to tell each other we wanted to play, as we did not have telephones. To make that whistle sound, we would put our hands together and blow between our thumbs. It sounded as if an owl was hooting.

One day, Billy's father was taking us to the ball game. We got a flat tire some three miles away from the game. Mr. Woodall proceeded to take the spare tire, which was also flat, and roll it towards our destination in hopes of finding a garage. Some of my team members saw us waiting in the car and stopped to pick me up, as I was the pitcher, and they thought the chances of winning the game depended on me. They did not have room for Billy so we left him behind. I felt very bad about this and wished later that I had stayed with my friend.

My brother Danny and Augie also played Little League and we were all on different teams. All three of us excelled in baseball and always made the All Stars and got to compete at District competition. In small rural areas, Little League games were a main source of entertainment for many people. Also, the community as a whole took the game very seriously. Although my father never said anything to us about the games, we often would see his blue pickup somewhere in the park observing when we played.

I played one year in the Pony League. My brother Paul and his wife Lourdes would take me to the game, as it was in the city of Lubbock some distance away.

I played football in Junior High, and, although our team was not very good, I d managed to score a few touchdowns. I really enjoyed this and thought I would play in high school. However, most of my teammates grew taller over the summer, and I guess I had already finished growing. Also, Apá was pressuring me to contribute more to the family by picking cotton after school. I felt obligated to work because I considered myself lucky to be allowed to go to high school. Looking back, probably my father would have allowed me to play football if I had been more assertive. I was glad, however, that my younger brother Danny was allowed to play high school football. He was a very good player and made All District.

My immediate friends were no longer the jocks, but people interested in music. Claud Hamaker, a classmate of mine whose father played the guitar, was instrumental in encouraging me to pursue my dream of playing. I remember that he got an electric guitar for Christmas. Claud loaned it to me for one weekend, and for those three days I pretended that it was mine. I had a ball, and I will never forget this gesture of kindness. He and I remained close friends all through high school and through our freshman year of college. To this day, one of my greatest pleasures is playing the guitar.

Don't Stop The Music

Written by Noé Lara
May 9, 2007

Sometimes the music is so soft,
only a whisper can be heard.
It touches our soul and tempers our mood,
As we seek answers for the absurd.

Sometimes the rhythmic tone,
Grows hollow and obscene.
Sometimes one conjures visions,
Of themes of the unseen.

Oh but let the music continue,
Let the bells and cymbals chime.
Don't stop the music for me yet,
This gift is yours as well as mine.

Don't stop the music quite just now,
From the orchestra and from the band.
Let those notes from singers wail,
Feelings we may never understand.

How many times have we been down,
While other times we celebrate.
Music is for every occasion,
To our soul it opens the gate.

¿CUÁNTAS PÍSCAS?

After school, Danny and I would be picked up by Apá and taken to the fields to pick cotton. I liked picking cotton, as it provided me an opportunity to make a little extra money. What I made after school went to help out at home. If we worked on Saturday or Sunday, Apá would tell us that we could keep our earnings. When arriving from school on the bus, we would see Apa's blue pick-up truck waiting to take us to the work site. Before we left, he would give us a chance to snack. Usually, our snack consisted of a tortilla filled with *frijoles boludos* (whole beans).

Picking cotton in West Texas was called "pulling bolls". In some parts of the state, workers would literally pick the cotton out of the bolls. In West Texas, we pulled the whole bolls, and the gins would separate the cotton later. We would wear cotton gloves similar to those worn by gardeners. Also, we always wore long sleeve shirts to protect our arms. However, sometimes the shirts were tattered so we still got our arms scratched. We would pull the bolls and put them in a long canvas sack that we would drag between two rows. The sacks were either twelve or fourteen feet long and had straps that fit around our shoulders.

Depending on how tightly we stuffed the cotton, we could conceivably put as much as two hundred pounds in a sack. We would then drag it to the *romana* (scale), which was attached to a twelve foot high tripod made from three 2X6 pieces of lumber. We would weigh the cotton sack, and my father would record the amount in a book. We would then hoist the sack up a trailer, usually putting it on our backs and walking up the ladder onto the trailer. At the end of the week Apá would tally up everyone's totals and pay the workers accordingly. I was always amazed at how he kept dozens of entries and could figure out what he owed people. Apá had no formal education, but he knew math well enough that he was able to do this fairly and accurately.

On some mornings it would be too wet to pick cotton, as fog or light rains had fallen during the night. Men would congregate, waiting for my father to give the word that the cotton was dry enough to pick. Sometimes they would play *wachas*, as they waited. Large washers were used for this game. We would throw them, with each player attempting to put his washer in a small hole that was dug for that purpose. It was a little like horseshoes. Many times, however, my father and the workers would just lean against the house or barns and visited, enjoying *la resolana* (heat of the morning sun).

Working in the cotton fields, usually in late September through November, was very cold. We would scratch our hands and arms with the cotton stalks, even though we wore gloves and long sleeves. Cotton off the stalk was usually very dirty, and the dust would accumulate in our nose, eyes, and mouth. It was very uncomfortable. Still, not only did it provide us the opportunity to help the family but also a chance to compete. My father frowned at the possibility that another kid my age could beat me picking cotton, so I strived to never let anyone my age beat me.

I was not as good as my older brothers David and Estévan, but I was still pretty good at picking cotton. I was able to pick as much as twelve hundred pounds in one day. Given that the average person can only pick six hundred pounds per day, this was significant. As I got a little older, I was recruited to work for my brother-in-law Sotero while he stripped cotton. Instead of picking cotton, a stripper machine was dragged behind a tractor along with a trailer. I stood in the back of the trailer and, with a pick, moved the cotton that had been stripped to the back of the trailer to accommodate more cotton. The weather was usually very cold, and my mouth and nose would fill with cotton and dirt.

La Písca

June 23, 2006

"La pisca de algodon" (Cotton Picking),
was hard work and little fun.
You'd cut your hands and scratch your eyes.
So glad when the day was done.

My father's blue pick-up truck,
"la troquita de Apa".
Would be waiting for us after school,
he would call us, "ven aca" (come here).

He would take us to the cotton fields,
but first a taco we would eat.
The weather many times was bitter cold,
It was like we had frozen hands and frozen feet.

You could make some extra money,
if your hands were strong and fast.
You hoped that your back hold up,
and that the day you'd last.

There were some good times,
but few and far between.
Maybe we did have fun,
More often we thought that the world was just plain mean.

We pulled our sacks,
headed for the scale.
Apá weighed our cotton,
to add to the bale.

Sometimes your sack weighed such,
You felt your sack could break the scale.
Other times we weren't as lucky,
When we picked at the speed of a snail.

"La pisca de algodon",
wasn't for sissy's you see.
At least it wasn't
for my family and me.

¿CUÁNTAS PÍSCAS?

It was while doing this kind of work that I arrived at a pivotal moment in my life. I strained my back and experienced excruciating pain. I was about 15 years old. This had happened once before. I came to the conclusion that if my livelihood and that of my family, should I be lucky enough to have one, depended on my doing this kind of work, I would not be very successful. From this moment forward, I began making plans to go to college in hopes of graduating and finding a job that did not require using my back to the extent that I had. As an adult, I would have problems which required herniated disk surgery. The doctor said that the kind of labor I performed when young contributed greatly to my bad back.

In the summer, I found myself either irrigating or chopping cotton. When I still was too young to be hired full time, I would help my brother David or Apá with the irrigation. This was when I was between 10 and 14 years of age. Mr. Adamson would give me twenty dollars at the end of the year so I could buy clothes for school. I also enjoyed him taking me and either David or Apá to a nearby gas station for a break. Mr. Adamson would buy us an Almond Joy candy bar and a Coca Cola. The Cokes at the time came in very small bottles, but they were nice and cold. This made me feel very good and much appreciated. It also made me feel guilty because I felt that I should be working, instead of enjoying the treats.

Irrigation wells were in every large field. They provided water that would travel through irrigation ditches or aluminum pipes to the rows of cotton. My job was to make sure that the water was directed at the rows of cotton growing in the fields and, when those rows were soaked, to move the water to another set of rows. Sometimes we would have to cross ditches full of water. We would get a running start and plunge the shovel in the ditch and whirl ourselves across. The first time I did this, I fell in. Apá, who was present, told me to not let the ditch win. I had to practice jumping the ditch until I was able to clear the water without falling in. The job required that we work from 7:00 a.m. to 7:00 p.m. Sometimes, it was also necessary to work at night. For this we were compensated $7 per day.

Chopping cotton was very tiring and boring work. If you did not have an imagination to carry you mentally away from the labor, you might get bored to death. We would walk between two rows of cotton chopping weeds away from the little cotton plants. Many times, the temperature would be well over one hundred degrees. I would usually wear jeans and gloves, and I always sported sunglasses and a straw cowboy hat. We would walk to the end of the row, turn back and, when we arrived at the car again, we could drink water and sharpen our hoes with a file. Sometimes Apá would sharpen our hoes for us.

One day, instead of chopping between two rows, I took six rows and chopped very fast. I saw the farmer that I worked for doing this. Apá let me do this for awhile, and then he sat down to talk to me. He said that I was going to wear myself out. He said that the farmer was underpaying us to begin with, and when he chopped cotton like that, he was not doing a good job. He was leaving a lot of weeds and that job probably would have to be re-done. He told me that the farmer owned the farm and had a personal incentive to do as much as he possibly could. He was not working like this ten hours a day and for five days a week, like we were. I learned that day to pace myself when working hard all day.

Because of the extreme heat, many times we would pray for a cloud in the sky to block the heat of the sun. We would imagine that there was a man in the sky, who we called *Barbas de Oro* (golden beard). It was indeed refreshing when Barbas de Oro would honor us with a cool shade, if only for a few moments at a time.

Apá was always the time keeper, telling us when it was time to go to lunch or go home. Sometimes, to make time pass faster, he would tell us that it was still a couple of hours before we could go home. Of course, we would moan about this. Then in about ten minutes, he would tell us that it was time to go. We would then learn that he had just been joking with us in an attempt to make us feel better. We felt great that we did not have to wait as long as we thought that we might. Apá would also help time pass by telling us stories from the Bible. Sometimes he would tell us a story that would be continued until after lunch or the next day. We always looked forward to his stories, and I was always amazed at how much he knew about the Bible.

¿CUÁNTAS PÍSCAS?

Most of the time, we would earn sixty cents an hour while we worked ten hours a day, from 7:00 a.m. to 6:00 p.m. Some farmers paid less than that. We enjoyed going home to lunch, but when we worked too far away to go home, we would take our lunches. When we did go home for lunch, we were so tired and hungry that it did not matter what we ate, we devoured it. I still remember the smell of *papas* (potatoes) with onions and tortillas as we approached our casita (little house). When I took a lunch, my favorite was flour tortillas with *frijoles dorados* (refried beans) and Spam and, for a drink, a Coke or orange Kool-Aid. In the evening, sometimes I would be so tired that I wasn't even hungry. I just wanted to drink a lot of water or Kool-Aid, and go to sleep.

Barbas de Oro

April 7, 2006

Barbas de oro,
I implore you shade me from this burning sun.
Let me feel the cool Spring breeze
as I toil with my *asadon (hoe).*

You are recognizable far above,
as you move about the sky.
You are my friend with the golden beard,
hurry up, I'm about to die!

As I contemplate my life,
as I move from row to row.
Let me feel that you are with me,
you are, is that not so?

Now I see you moving slowly,
with your friends the friendly clouds.
I can feel your soothing *sombra (shadow),*
forgive me for my doubts.

Barbas de Oro you were with me,
when in vain I sought relief.
Thank you for *tu sombrita (little shade),*
though at times oh so brief.

¿CUÁNTAS PÍSCAS?

While chopping cotton, I would often look up at the sky when I would hear the sound of a plane engine. I would see airplanes flying by and would wonder where they were going and what kind of people had the luxury to fly anywhere they desired. Later in life, when I got a job with a national housing corporation in Washington D.C., I was able to fly all over the country as part of my duties. I would look down at communities below, and I would wonder what kind of folks were down below and what they must be up to. I surmised that there were probably still many people down there who were chopping cotton as I once did.

I also had opportunities to plow on the farm. My father would instruct me to aim at a particular object when plowing, and I would be able to keep my rows straight. I usually would aim at a tree or a house in the distance. How straight you plowed your rows was a source of much pride.

I had other opportunities to work driving a tractor. After a good rain, it wasn't unusual to see the wind blow and farmers scrambling to fight the sand. Sandfighting was the process of dragging a wide apparatus with a tractor. This contraption consisted of a series of pointy objects resembling railroad spikes. The holes that the sandfighter made served to slow down soil erosion caused by strong winds which often accompanied a good rain.

Meanwhile, I continued my education. I always tried to be a good citizen in school and worked hard at not getting into trouble. Looking back, however, I can see that my attempts to be more sociable or to be like other kids who seemed to be having a lot of fun, failed because I felt that someone would always remind me that I wasn't supposed to have fun

While most of my school experiences were positive, there were occasions when they were not so pleasant. In the seventh grade, while everyone was supposed to be quiet and studying, I remarked out loud that it had started raining. The teacher told me that I had to stay after school and write a couple of pages from the dictionary because I had disrupted the class. I felt this punishment unfair and a total waste of time. I told my teacher that I lived about seven miles from school and that I couldn't stay after school because I had to take the bus home.

She said that I could satisfy the penalty by taking a licking. I agreed to this. I also had never had a licking and wanted to know what it felt like. She asked that I take everything out of my back pockets and bend over. She hit me with a wooden paddle seven times. It hurt like the dickens and it was very humiliating.

On another occasion, when I was in study hall a Latino friend of mine, who drew a lot of negative attention by acting funny, was making a great deal of noise. The monitor, who was a coach, looked at me and made me move from where I was sitting and embarrassed me in front of everyone. I tried to tell him that it wasn't me who was making noise, but he refused to listen. At the end of the class, he looked at me and said, "You were right. It wasn't you I meant to punish." He offered no apology for embarrassing me and making me feel so bad.

On another occasion, during a Physical Education class, we were playing basketball. I didn't go out for the team because I did not like to wear shorts. Also, I did not feel that I was good enough. This time we were playing a pretty intense game. I was in my zone and made several baskets in a row. It seemed to me that I could not miss! I thought that the coach was going to notice this and encourage me to join the regular team. Instead, he belittled me for trying to show off and offered no words of encouragement. I never tried hard again and gave up illusions of ever being recognized for my athletic abilities.

While in junior high, I participated in football and therefore was somewhat accepted. My team mates would sometimes say, "You are not like the rest." In other words, I wasn't like the rest of the Latino kids who apparently were looked down upon. I don't know if this was supposed to make me feel good, but I sure didn't take it that way. I remember a time when a bus load of migrant boys were getting off a bus. Some of the Anglo kids that I was with decided to pick a fight with them. When the ruckus started, by instinct I started fighting on the side of the Mexican migrant kids. One of my Anglo friends asked me why I sided against them. I couldn't explain it because I myself did not understand it.

¿CUÁNTAS PÍSCAS?

During the first few years of school and before entering high school, I grew very sensitive to the way Hispanic students were treated. I tried very hard to adhere to all of the rules so I could be spared unnecessary criticism. Although this kept me from becoming more sociable, I believe that it contributed to my academic success.

Car being hoisted and pushed. Wisconsin Near Tragedy

Apa-Writers father

Noe batting, brother Danny catching

8th Grade football team. (Noe #82)

CHAPTER 6

A Home of our Own

The summer before I was to start the ninth grade, we moved. Apá and my brother Paul had jointly purchased a twelve-acre parcel of land a couple of years before, with the intention of eventually building our own house. As it turned out, we found a house-to-be-moved in the newspaper and began exploring the possibility of buying that structure. We went to see the building, which was a very big Victorian-style house. At least it was big compared to the one we had been living in. The cost was high and, after adding what it would cost to move it and build a foundation to set the house on, we gave up on the idea. Much later, the house was still on the market, and Apá asked me to inquire about it again. Apá used me as his translator as we negotiated with the realtor, whose name was Buddy Hughes. The price had dropped, making it feasible for us to buy it.

The house was moved some twenty miles from East Lubbock to the "twelve acres," as often called the property. They had a difficult time, and all of us, including the movers, were starting to doubt if it would make it to its destination. It took them more than two weeks to get the house to the twelve acres. Apparently, the mover had to have several phone lines cut because the house roof was very high. He also complained because he had gotten several traffic violations along the way. The last leg had him cutting across a cotton field and over a couple of ditches because that was the only way to get it where it was supposed to go.

Once there, it gave all of us a wonderful sense of pride because it was a four bedroom house with a nice roomy attic that eventually was converted to bedrooms. We began buying material, and we would work on it in the evenings and weekends. We painted it and finished the wrap-around porches. My brother David built a brick enclosure on the foundation to prevent the plumbing from freezing.

The house had a large porch on the west side that wrapped around to the south. It also had a porch in the back that opened to the kitchen. Inside it had a large dining area that later became the center of our social activities. The front door opened directly into the living room from the west side of the house.

I now enjoyed my own room. Also, we were no longer ashamed to have friends over. I remember that my friends would come over and could not believe that we owned this big house. Their first thoughts were that we lived on some Anglo's farm, and they had provided us with the house. When we lived at the other house, we were always embarrassed to let friends know where we lived.

We had already built a well, so it wasn't difficult hooking up the plumbing. We built a septic tank and hooked up the electricity. So after so many years, we finally had indoor plumbing, and we could say goodbye to hauling water as we had done for so many years. This was the first time that I experienced indoor plumbing at home. It took my father several weeks before he could work up the courage to use the restroom inside the house. He said that somehow, it just didn't seem right. The cold weather eventually became the motivator for my father to get used to the luxury of indoor plumbing.

At the twelve acres, we were able to raise hogs and occasionally would butcher one and have a *matanza*. Relatives and friends would come to help us kill, shave, and butcher the hog. We would, of course, make some delicious *chicharones* (pork rinds). My father, who was an excellent butcher, directed the operation. When my sister married my brother-in-law Joe, Apá turned over his duties to him because Joe was also a good butcher, and Apá saw himself growing too old to handle the job. This activity brought a lot of joy to all of us, and we always looked forward to the matanzas.

Apá started raising chickens on our property. But, there were more chicken hawks on the twelve acres than at our other house. We were constantly watching to insure that they didn't swoop down and take our egg-laying hens. One day, one was swooping down, and Apá took out his twelve-gauge shotgun and blew it out of the sky. I was truly amazed at his accuracy. The hawk was so beautiful that I wished that he didn't like eating our chickens so he wouldn't have to be killed.

I always admired the banty hens that a neighbor raised. They were short and had feathers all the way down to their feet. I proposed to the neighbor that I trade our chickens for his, and he agreed. I caught our chickens and took them over to his farm for the exchange. I was very proud of my deal until Apá came home. I had neglected to tell him what I was going to do. I guess it just slipped my mind! Anyway, he was very angry, as I had traded his egg-laying hens for tiny chickens that, if they would lay eggs, the eggs would probably be the size of a BB. On top of it all, I did not get a rooster in the trade, so the little hens could not even lay eggs. Apá finally calmed down and found a little banty rooster. His *compadre* José Arredondo happened to have one and gave it to him. In a few days, the hens started laying these cute tiny eggs.

We also built a storm cellar, a must if you live in West Texas. In the spring, it is not unusual to spot tornadoes, either in the sky or on the ground. Our hand-dug cellar was small, about eight feet by ten feet, and about eight feet deep. The walls were lined with brick and the top was a concrete slab. The family was blessed because we never had to use the cellar in a storm. At the Adamson farm, we also had a storm cellar, and we did have to use it several times. We had been fortunate that a tornado had never touched the ground and damaged that house.

My sister Marta and her husband bought a little house and put it on the twelve acres, so they lived there long before we did. Later, they built a bigger house, as their family was growing. My brother Steve and his bride Lupe moved into the smaller house for a while. Later still, my brother Augie married and built a house next to Marta's house. When Danny got out of the military, and he married, he and his wife Cissy built a house. It was a big beautiful house with a double car garage, better than any one of us had ever owned.

I remember telling Danny that he had became *el Viejo* (the old man). We always referred to the Anglo bosses, who usually had big beautiful houses, as the viejos. Danny had just joined the ranks! Danny's house was just a stone's throw from the house where we grew up in, Amá's house, as it was later called. There is a great big fruitless mulberry tree between the two houses. Over the years, this tree has provided a lot of fun for the Lara grandchildren. Their childhoods are well-documented by Danny as he took their pictures, and show the photos to them when they got older. The well is also located between the two houses.

When we bought the house, in the attic were several old newspapers dating back to the early 1900's. We also found an American flag with forty-eight stars. We guessed that the flag, was probably given to the original owners by the military to honor a deceased soldier in their family. The house also came with a house guest. Many in our family have seen a woman dressed in white who walked from the well to the house porch. She has also been seen inside in various parts of the house.

I personally have never seen this ghost. However, one time as I took my turn caring for my mother when my sister Connie was at work as a night nurse at the local hospital, I was awakened by a strong smell of roses. I thought nothing of it, thinking that my mother must have taken a bath and used some lotion or powder that smelled like roses. However, I walked over to her room to check on her and found that this was not the case. This happened to me twice. So I may not have seen this ghost, but I have certainly sensed her strong presence!

Lara family home located in Lubbock, Texas

CHAPTER 7

High School Years

I strived to retain the knowledge provided in high school and many times became frustrated that I could not always do so. While in high school, I always worked towards perfection, but rationalized that I had plenty of time should I not immediately achieve it. Although teachers and classmates told me that I was a bright student, I never really believed it. I just thought I was very lucky that I could make good grades. My shy nature and my insecurity led me to interact with people at the most superficial level. I learned social skills to get me by, but always felt that someday someone was going to expose me as a fraud.

Although I never volunteered for anything, when I was drafted for a task, I would rise to the occasion. For example, as a freshman in high school I was nominated by my classmates to represent them in the "most handsome" contest. The ordeal was very painful for me. It was painful because firstly, I didn't think I was the most handsome and secondly, because I did not have the proper clothes to wear for the contest. Eventually, my mother and my married sister Marta were able to get me a pair of black pants, and I borrowed a white sports jacket from a classmate.

I did not win and was glad. The attention that the winner received would have been more than I could have handled. On the plus side, the experience helped me to realize that I was actually capable of getting through such an ordeal. I concluded that challenges might seem temporarily painful, but, in order to grow, I needed to experience more of them.

In high school I also belonged to the Spanish Club and participated in interscholastic activities. One year, my partner and I were selected as the King and Queen of a District Fiesta. My sister Marta made my dance costume. She and my mother went to a thrift shop where they bought me a pair of white painters' pants. They then took an ordinary old white shirt and put ruffles on it to resemble a dancer's shirt. They put a bright purple sash across my waist, and I wore an old straw sombrero. My partner, Janice Stewart, was from an Air Force family. She was very pretty and smart, and it was a joy to work with her. That same year, I also won a first place ribbon for reciting a poem in Spanish.

The next year we competed in San Antonio. I was again successful, winning a couple of ribbons. For the San Antonio trip, I remember borrowing a shirt from my brother Paul. The shirt was a little big, but I was very limited in my wardrobe. Paul always had good taste in the clothes that he wore. The trips helped boost my confidence, as no one in my family had ever done anything like this before.

Because of the persistence and hard work of civil rights groups and the leadership of men like Dr. Martin Luther King, Jr., schools in the South were one by one being integrated. The winds of change came to our small rural school during my sophomore year. I still remember the day that a young black student named C.L. Harris walked down the halls of Frenship High accompanied by the superintendent. The rumors had already spread that this was going to happen, but no one believed it until they actually saw it. All lessons stopped for a few brief moments as even the teachers were curious about this different student that they would be teaching. Doors were opened toward the hallway, and everyone stretched their necks as far as they could to witness this historic moment. Unlike other schools, and except for a few sneers and bad jokes, pretty soon everything was back to normal. Like the Mexican-American students who fought hard for their right to an education, despite existing prejudices, C.L. managed to adjust in our school without too many interruptions as far as I know.

When The Winds of Change Came to Frenship High
Written By Noé Lara
March 2007

Holy Spirit, Holy Smoke,
Holy winds of time,
C.L. Harris came and went,
let's have a glass of wine.

He brought the wind of change,
The bus delivered him to the door.
First there were sneers, and then there were jokes,
And then there was no more.

He came to visit with his dark sad soul,
I am sure he didn't mean to stay.
But when they saw he wasn't a threat,
He never went away.

They got used to this strange black kid,
He wasn't like all of the rest.
C.L. played a little football,
Coach said he was one of the best.

There were others after him,
dozens as a matter of fact.
But there is no doubt that he paved the way,
He was lead man on this inevitable track.

¿CUÁNTAS PÍSCAS?

He made friends in this West Texas school,
Seemed like people gave him a chance.
Like us he enjoyed a little rock'n roll,
He even sang at the school dance.

Where were the Chicanos in all of this,
When the winds of change came down?
We were used to being in our place,
We acted serious or the class clown.

We fought hard to be invisible,
To stay under the radar screen. C.L.
Harris helped me too,
They turned their attention on him.

Cesar Chavez had his cause,
Farmworkers like my daddy and me.
Martin Luther took it further,
He marched in Memphis Tennessee.

C.L. came to Frenship High, In 1963.
He brought thé winds of change with him,
Shared his dignity for all of us to see.

Because I was shy, I didn't date much in junior high. In high school, I didn't date many girls because it was a small school, and most of the good-looking girls were already taken. It was also difficult because we lived so far from school, and I did not usually have access to a car.

I was a junior when I finally got a car of my own. However, I could only drive it to work and back. My father I bought me a 1958 Renault 4CV. It was a very small blue car with a water-cooled engine in the back. The car was designed to be cranked in the event that the battery gave out. It had a bad tendency to overheat and eventually this caused the engine to go.

I would often go into town with friends that I knew from church Henry and his brother Pete. We would cruise downtown looking for girls.

I did manage to find a girlfriend. Emma was very pretty. She had long light brown hair and green eyes. Emma came from a racially- mixed family. Her father was a Latino and her mother was Anglo. She was funny and witty. We had a wonderful time together until one day, when I went out of town, she dated one of my friends. This ended our relationship. Emma was the first girl that I had been intimate with.

While I attended high school, I had jobs other than farm work. The summer after my sophomore year, I got a job at Reese Air Force Base as a bus boy at the Officers Club. The base was located some seven miles from where we lived. I will never forget Apá's reaction when I told him I wanted to work somewhere other than at the farm. He told me that I was not going to be treated right at the base and reminded me that I already had a good job. He tried to discourage me from what I perceived to be an opportunity. Looking back, I can see that he was only trying to protect me from the unfair and sometimes vicious world that he had experienced. Apá was trying to shelter me in the only way that he knew how.

I worked all summer and actually got very good at washing dishes and busing tables. I made friends, and management offered me a permanent job. However, I already had dreams of going to college and knew that I did not want to do this job for the rest of my life. I returned to school after the summer but this experience, helped me realize that I could do jobs other than farm work.

The summer before my senior year in high school, I heard of summer jobs for disadvantaged students. I applied at the State Employment Office and got a job with the Bureau of Reclamation. They were building a water line between Amarillo, which is located in the panhandle of Texas, to Lamesa, Texas, some 150 miles to the south. The Canadian River Project was an experiment that would transfer water from the Canadian River to be used by communities in West Texas that were expected to experience droughts in the future.

I was a pipe inspector. The 36 and 52 inch round concrete pipes were built in Lubbock, tested, and then transferred to the site. The job of the engineers was to inspect the pipe, survey the line, and supervise the project. I was small enough to crawl inside the pipes by riding on my back on a flat cart with wheels, similar to those used by mechanics to work under cars. I wore a hard hat with a lamp on it, and I had a large marker that I would use when I found a crack in the pipes. Construction men would then repair the pipe before shipping it out. This was a rewarding working experience, as I was constantly told that I was doing a good job. I was also encouraged by the engineers to major in engineering when I attended college.

Comfort Zone

June 23, 2006

Sometimes we get so comfortable,
in our little world of friends.
We dare not cross the road,
meet strangers or to take a chance.

We need not be so careful,
or be afraid to make a mistake.
We should explore and question,
And perhaps a risk to take.

We will never know what's out there,
if we don't take a chance.
Start a quest for something new,
try to learn a different dance.

So what if there is danger out there,
crooks, wild critters or a storm?
We will learn to protect ourselves,
find our fortune, or learn to stay warm.

What's wrong with a little adventure,
it can only make us strong.
We'll meet people that can help us grow,
if we get out of our comfort zone.

¿CUÁNTAS PÍSCAS?

The summer after high school graduation, I got a job with a local farmer who was building a tomato green house. This was a new business venture for Mr. Jones. We were to construct the green house and then work planting, cultivating, and harvesting the tomatoes. My family had worked for Mr. Jones in the past, and I remembered that he paid us less than any other farmer in the area. I was at first reluctant to take this job because of his reputation.

I felt very inadequate, as I worked alongside mature men who were stronger and certainly knew a lot more about construction than I did. At the same time, I was paid $1.25 an hour, one whole quarter more than these experienced men were getting paid. Although I appreciated this, I felt very awkward with the situation. Mr. Jones was trying to help me save enough money because he knew that I was college-bound. The difference in our wages was later found out, which caused a big commotion with the men, particularly one who was labeled as a trouble-maker. All the men were then given a raise.

I later felt justified in getting the extra quarter for the time that I did, because of an idea that I contributed that saved Mr. Jones both time and money. We had been rot-proofing the lumber that was used for construction by putting copper sulphate on the beams, using an ordinary paint brush. This consumed a great deal of labor and time. I asked Mr. Jones whether I could call my high school chemistry teacher for some advice. After I described the situation, the teacher suggested that we cut one or two 55-gallon drums in half, and weld them together. We could then fill them with copper sulphate and just dunk the lumber into the vats. Mr. Jones liked the idea and we did just that. He did save a lot of time and money. Later, I worked in the tomato greenhouse actually doing greenhouse work.

Noe & Janice crowned King and Queen of Regional Festival

Noe upon graduating from Frenship High School

CHAPTER 8

Texas Tech Bound, 1964-1969

Double T

My aspirations to go to college had begun when I was a freshman in high school. I was confident that I had the grades to succeed. My school was not accustomed to encouraging Hispanics to go to college, and I was no exception. In fact, in my senior year when all my classmates were signed up to take the SAT, I was not even told about it. I showed up for school one day and all of my classmates were gone. I inquired about this and was told that were taking their SAT tests, and they assumed that I was not interested in going to college. I later took the test on my own!

A year before, I had asked the school counselor about college and particularly a school in Albuquerque, New Mexico. He discouraged me, telling me that my parents would not be able to afford to send me to any school. He even went as far as to tell me, "Look at the way you are dressed. It takes money to attend college." He did not inform me of scholarships or other ways to afford college. Interestingly enough, this same person called to congratulate me when I graduated from Texas Tech. However, and almost in the same breath, he tried to sell me life insurance, as he was now in the life insurance business. He had seen my name in the local newspaper along with the names of all of the other Texas Tech graduates. My first thought was that perhaps he should have been selling insurance instead of unfairly counseling kids like me.

A former pastor of mine told me about a Methodist Church Sunday school class that was looking for Hispanic high school students who had good grades and were interested in attending Texas Tech University. I applied for the scholarship, was interviewed, and was selected. The interview was one of the most embarrassing times in my life.

I had no idea how to prepare for the important interview. I bought a very inexpensive suit at a low budget store. The pant legs were at least an inch longer than they needed to be. When I arrived at the Sunday school president's house, I quickly learned that it was a backyard swimming and barbeque party. No one had bothered to tell me, and I did not know enough to ask how I was to dress. I sweated bullets throughout the evening. To top it off, the host showed slides about his recent vacation in Acapulco, Mexico. I could not remotely identify with any of what was going on there.

I got through the evening, and I got the scholarship. It could have been because they felt sorry for me and how uncomfortable the whole ordeal had been for me. I was granted a four- year scholarship, which included expenses related to supplies and books.

The scholarship was contingent on my getting passing grades. One member of the Sunday school class was a partner in a bookstore near campus. He offered me a job and promised flexibility in my work schedule to accommodate my taking off to attend classes. I worked in this bookstore for a couple of years. I will forever be indebted to the St. John's Methodist Church Sunday school class.

College was not anything like high school. The university had a very large campus, and no one seemed to care whether you attended classes or not. I remember that I would have nightmares about not finding my classroom. I went from attending a school that had forty-six senior students to a campus of over 25,000 people. Some of my classes had over three hundred students in them. I started by taking eighteen credit hours a semester but soon learned that doing this and working part time was just not feasible. I soon took fewer hours.

College was a fun place to be, and I soon grew in confidence and became more sociable. Unlike high school, I didn't know anyone, and no one knew me. It was like starting fresh. In high school there were many class distinctions, and there was a great deal of discrimination. In college there were dozens of Hispanic students and several nice, open-minded Anglos who I made friends with. Very definitely, there were some very pretty girls!

I remember the first time that I went to the Student Union Building (SUB). I was sitting looking toward the door when I saw this beautiful girl walk in. I did not know at the time that she was Hispanic, as she was very light-complexioned. Lo and behold, she started walking toward me. I thought that she would just go by me to her destination. I was surprised to learn that I was her destination. She stopped and introduced herself and then proceeded to ask questions in an attempt to get to know me. I was very nervous and perhaps she sensed it, as she worked to put me at ease. We became good friends, dating on and off for almost two years. Estelle was my first college sweetheart.

Estelle introduced me to a Latino university club called *Los Tertulianos* (the social people) It was a social organization where we could get together and talk about issues pertaining to Hispanics. There was still a lot of discrimination in Texas, and the club provided us with a forum for discussing civil rights and other issues of the day. I remember that one year we decided to participate in the Homecoming parade. We entered a float which actually was very attractive. I had been named the chairman of the float committee, so this project took a great deal of my time. We did not win the prize for the best float, but we caught the attention and respect of others at the University. I was elected the president of the club for the following year.

One of the courses that I took was Military Science. I was enrolled in the Air Force ROTC and was a member of the Saber Squad, a rifle-carrying marching drill team. I remember that every Thursday we had to wear our uniforms. I took the officer's exam, which was very lengthy and difficult, and I made a passing grade. However, I was not satisfied that I knew enough to be an Air Force officer.

This was the time of the Vietnam War, and the Army was also very aggressive in its recruitment on campus. Even though students would be wearing Air Force uniforms, Army recruiters would stop us and encourage us to switch to the Army. At their insistence, I took the Army's officers test. It took me about thirty minutes to take the exam, and I made a very high score. I concluded that at this time the Army was desperate for officers and their standards were probably lowered for this purpose. I was not swayed. I elected not to pursue a commission in the military, which had been one of my career options. As a sociology major, I had been following the Vietnam conflict and had begun see the futility of our efforts there and began to question the whole concept of war. I eventually dropped out of ROTC.

When I was a sophomore, my brother Danny joined me in attending Texas Tech. I remember that we would drive Apá's blue pick-up truck from the farm to school, which was about ten miles away. The truck did not have a heater so in the winter time we drove with our head out the window, as the windshield was frozen and we could not see ahead of us. A singing duo called the Righteous Brothers was very popular at the time. About the same time as we were going to school each morning, the radio would play one of their songs, which became my all-time favorite. The name of the song is "Soul and Inspiration."

Danny and I did not socialize together, as we had different friends. One day, after my father had bought another car which we had started using, I walked to the parking lot only to find our vehicle missing. I solicited the help of the campus police and returned to the SUB, telling my friends that someone had stolen my car. After a few minutes, Danny walked into the SUB and said, "Let's go". I proceeded to tell him that we could not, as someone had stolen our car. He told me that he had taken the car. Apparently he had had another key made. Even though I was very angry at the time, he and I laugh about this today. Soon afterwards, Danny was drafted into the army and eventually left for Vietnam.

I dated several girls who went to Tech and some that did not. It was easy getting dates, as any Hispanic going to college had the potential for being successful so was considered a good catch. The social activities usually included going to football games and parties. During the week we would just cruise downtown and in the park.

Lubbock was a dry county, so there were no liquor stores. There was, however, a strip of liquor stores located about ten miles from town. In fact, it was called "The Strip". Sometimes we would put together our quarters and dimes and go out to get a six pack. One of my friends and I could play the guitar a little. We would take his guitar, get a six pack and go to an isolated cotton fields to play music and drink beer. Usually there would be about six of us, both guys and gals, so we really did not drink all that much. All of us were under age at the time anyway.

I remember one time that we had just come from the The Strip with a six-pack of beer. It was in the evening and a little dark so we turned on the dome light to see to open the beer. At that time they did not have pull tabs, so we had to use a can opener. As one of us was opening a can, a Liquor Control Board agent who was driving by saw us. He stopped us and made us pour the beer out. He cited every one of us and gave us a court date. We showed up in court and the judge fined us thirty-five dollars each. Everyone paid up, but I did not have the money.

The judge said that I would have to do some jail time. I don't know if he was trying to scare me or whether he was serious. I asked him what time the court house closed, as I would go look for the money. He gave me until 5:00 p.m. to pay the fine. I was still working at the Varsity Book Store, so I asked my boss for an advance. He leant me the thirty-five dollars, and I went and paid my fine. Every day for weeks after that, I would look in the newspaper to see if there had been a police report on this incident, as I did not want any of my relatives to tell my parents. Luckily, they did not report it and to my knowledge my parents never found out. Since I had blown my weekly paycheck, for a few days my meals were only those I ate at home, as I was still living there at the time.

While in college, and after I left the bookstore, I got a part time job with the Neighborhood Youth Corp (NYC). This was a non-profit organization whose objective was to counsel disadvantaged young people and place them in working situations with local businesses. I really enjoyed this position and instead of the ninety cents an hour I was making at the bookstore, I was now making five dollars an hour.

To put it in perspective, working at the farm and chopping cotton, I would have been making six dollars working ten hours a day. I remember that my older brother David would proudly tell his friends who were visiting him at home that I was making five dollars an hour. There weren't too many people that we knew, especially in our family, who had ever made that much money per hour. He once jokingly said, "If I was making five dollars an hour, I would work two hours and go home."

I really enjoyed working for the NYC, as I had my own office, and I felt that I was really making a contribution to *la Causa* (the Cause). This is what we called the struggle of the Hispanic community to participate in the mainstream of society. Interestingly enough, many of these young people were not much younger than me.

While I worked with NYC, I was also recruited to run an after-school recreational program sponsored by the YWCA. I developed activities for the barrio kids. Swimming was the center of the activities. NYC and the YWCA programs brought me a sense of personal satisfaction because I felt I was doing well in the community, especially when most of my clients were Hispanic. At the same time, they were good-paying jobs.

At a party in my junior year, I met the girl who would become my wife. Enes was not attending Texas Tech, but a college in Dallas. At first there seemed to be no attraction, but soon I would see her with another friend who did attend Tech. At these chance encounters, we would talk. She was a little older than me and dressed very nicely. She was also driving a brand new Mustang. At first I thought that she was way out of my league. Nonetheless, after some time, we began dating.

One time we went to a party that she had been invited to and which was hosted by her hairdresser who also attended Texas Tech. It was around Christmas and I guess I had drank more than I should have. On the way back, we went off the road and onto a railroad track. The two front tires of her sixty-six Mustang, which I was driving, blew out. Someone stopped to help me put the spare tire on and to help us get the car back on the road. I drove the car with one tire flat for some six miles to where Enes lived and where I had left my car. I got in my car and drove home happy to be alive and safe, as I quickly sobered up.

I didn't call Enes for a while, as I thought she would be mad at me because of that foolish incident. Later I got a message from her that she was wondering why I had not called. We resumed dating. By this time, Enes had gotten a job in Lubbock and decided not to return to college in Dallas. After a while, we felt very good about each other, and both of us were ready to settle down. We decided to get married and soon after were looking forward to our first child. It was not easy being married and attending school, especially when you also had the responsibility of rearing a child. Fortunately, my side of the family was always willing to baby-sit and Enes had a pretty good job so we got by fairly well.

I was becoming involved in the community and I concluded that any work regarding advocacy for Latinos in our community would probably be better received if I was married. And in fact it was.

We lived in a couple of apartments before we bought our own house. With the help of a friend, who was also a member of the St. John's Sunday school class, we were able to get a mortgage.

College social life had just consumed all my free time. After marriage, I began to focus more on my studies. I remember that I just got used to attending college. One day one of my friends told me that he was graduating. I was surprised, because we had started college at the same time. He then told me to check my credits, and that I probably could also graduate. Sure enough, I had enough credits and I did graduate.

I don't know what I was expecting, but I was sorely disappointed that I did not feel any different upon graduation. Maybe it was because I never went through a formal cap and gown ceremony. I really didn't know how I was supposed to feel, but I was sure that I was supposed to feel differently. I was a little confused, and it wasn't until later that I fully grasped the importance of that college degree.

CHAPTER 9

Dream Realized, 1969-2005

I had been dreaming of this moment for over 16 years. I finally was going to get a job as a professional and with it came the opportunity to use the education and training received over the years. Those countless hours of studying at night and delaying gratification in so many ways was finally going to pay off.

My first job as a professional was with Child Protective Services (CPS) in Lubbock, Texas. It's an interesting story how I landed this job. Upon graduation from college, I found an ad in the *Avalanche Journal*, the local paper, advertising for a social worker. When I went to the State Employment office, there was a long line of graduates after the same job. Some of them were college classmates. I felt very insecure, and I did not plan on getting the job. However, because I was bilingual and they had never had a bilingual person, they selected me. For the first time I felt that my Mexican heritage was working for me instead of against me, like it had many times in the past.

Even though I had experience working with youth at NYC and YWCA, this job carried with it a great deal more responsibility. The families affected stood to lose their children. We had the potential of affecting their lives forever. I knew how much I loved my family and my family loved me, so I couldn't imagine what it would have been like if someone had separated me from my family when I was young. Since then I have observed many children who have been separated from their families because they either abused them or failed to protect them. The children feel either betrayed or abandoned by parents or care givers. The separation is many times emotional and traumatic. Many children are scared forever.

I was very excited about working with CPS of Lubbock County, as it had the potential of turning into a career. Because I was the first bi-lingual social worker hired by the county, I felt wanted, needed, and appreciated. Working in this job gave me a wonderful sense of accomplishment, as I could sense that clients liked me and staff appreciated that I was there. At first I was somewhat afraid of what clients would do when confronted with charges of child abuse. I shadowed a couple of experienced social workers who were very competent, and I modeled myself after them.

The CPS staff was very young and very open-minded. The supervisor, however, was a conservative man with racist tendencies. I remember long-haired young male client came into the office. He actually was a very smart teenager with a lot of problems because he had been neglected. The supervisor made this comment to him, "Get a haircut. I haven't ever known of anyone with long hair that ever amounted to anything." The teenager, without missing a beat, told him, "How about Jesus?" All of us broke out laughing, agreeing that our boss deserved that comeback.

On another occasion, this same supervisor inspected a child who was scheduled to be adopted and said that this child was not adoptable. The child was a pretty little Anglo boy who had been born cognitively normal. The supervisor inspected the child's fingernails and then proceeded to tell us that the child was African-American. He told us that you could always tell by looking at the cuticles of their fingers. If they were bright orange, then they were Black. I asked my Anthropology instructor whether this was an accurate way of knowing, and she told me that it was not. In those days, mixed-blood children could not be adopted by Anglo families in Texas.

About the time I started working for CPS, there had been a shooting in one of the high schools in Lubbock. The victim was an African-American student. Discrimination toward both Blacks and Hispanics was high at the time. In response to the shooting, Blacks elected to take to the streets, forcing the city to impose a curfew. I had always sided with the Blacks because many times we seemed to be in the same boat. As a matter of fact, when we traveled south to visit my married sister Chila in Caldwell, we would stop on the way to get some barbeque. There was a community that was known to make the best barbeque and sausage in the world. The establishments had signs indicating where the whites and where the African-Americans could sit to eat their barbeque. I knew that I could sit in the white side, but I always felt more comfortable eating with the African-American families.

At one point during the time of the riots in Lubbock, I was on my way to make a home visit in one of the housing projects. I saw a group of African-American men staring at me, but I had no idea they had any intention of harming me. One of the clients I was to see ran out toward me with her friend and took me by the arm into the apartment. They sensed that I was in danger and ran to protect me. They talked to the men and told them that I was there to help them. They also accompanied me to my car when I left.

I guess because I was wearing a suit and a tie I represented authority, which mostly Anglos had at the time. This was the first time that I felt I was on the other side of a minority issue, even though my sympathy was with the African-Americans for the way they were being treated in the United States. Racial tension continued to be high for quite a while.

I recall several cases that taught me some profound lessons as a new social worker. One time I was working with a woman who was in her early forties and who had a thirteen-year old daughter. This mother was expecting a baby and had a lot of anguish over her situation because she was a single mom, and the expected child's father had abandoned her. She was exceedingly depressed and overwhelmed with her situation. I worked with her for a couple of months and became convinced that her best solution lay in her giving up the baby for adoption. I convinced her of this and explained the process that would take place.

I told her that the baby would go to a good home and to people that had the money and the time to provide for it. The mother agreed.

When it came time for delivery, I was called to the hospital. I invited a notary, so we could immediately take custody of the child. This was the only way that the county would pay for the delivery. When the mother saw her beautiful baby, she just could not go through with the plan. She elected to keep the little girl, and frankly, I was glad that she did.

We had developed a very close relationship and she insisted that I name the baby. I named the baby *Estrella*, which means star. After the child was born, the mother started feeling better about life and didn't need me as much. I then started prioritizing other families on my caseload. A few weeks later, someone at the office told me that the mother was frantically looking for me because the baby was sick.

In the Mexican culture, many people believe in *el ojo*. In many cultures this is simply referred to as the evil eye. It is the belief that some people have the power to gaze at someone, either a child or an adult, and, if they have envy in their heart, it could cause the person they looked at to get sick. I grew up believing that some people can make a child sick if they find that child exceptionally pretty and if they do not touch the child's face. The mother also had this belief and wanted me to go to her home and touch the child so that this ojo influence would go away. I did and it did. I am not sure that I completely believed in the ojo, but she certainly did. After this experience, I have been very careful to touch children on the face if I find them to be exceptionally pretty. Just in case!

Another memorable case was when I was assigned to talk to a mother of four who was reported for prostitution, possibly neglecting or compromising her children. When I arrived at her apartment, I found her to be a very amiable lady, and her children appeared to be well-loved and cared for. She told me her story.

She had been put in jail for several months for shoplifting. She had done this to get food for her children. She suffered a great deal because she was away from them. Now, and only once in a while, she would sell her body. She told me that she wasn't proud of this fact and only did it when she could not make ends meet. Also, she knew that there was not a heavy penalty for this. In fact, she told me that she knew a lawyer who could get her out of jail by paying a $50 fine.

She could then resume taking care of her children. She had a plan for her sister to take the kids whenever she was arrested. Her sister could do this on a short term care basis only. I could not find it in myself to find her at fault for trying her best with the reality of life that she faced.

After I worked for CPS for about a year, I was recruited by the Division of Vocational Rehabilitation (DVR) to start a school for their clients. The school was designed to provide remedial education while building the students' self esteem. The goal was to prepare them for continued vocational education or to enter the job market. Most of the students came from the DVR caseload but some came from the welfare rolls and Adult Probation. Many of the students were on medication to help with depression or anxiety issues. Most of the students were women. The class consisted of students who were Hispanic, African-American, and Anglo.

While working with these clients, I encountered many sad situations. One student, who I will call Angie, was a short, petite Hispanic woman with a patch of gray hair above her forehead. She was very pleasant and was an average student. It was my custom to go to work early to prepare for the day. She surprised me one day by coming in early, way before the other students. She walked into my office with a small brown paper bag that I took to be her lunch. She seemed a little nervous as she opened the bag and pulled out a small twenty-two caliber pearl handle pistol. I was surprised and a little fearful of her intent. She became very nervous, and it seemed to me that she was waving the pistol around. I tried not to appear nervous, but I could feel myself shaking. I talked to her for a bit, attempting to persuade her to hand me the gun. She moved her hand nervously but eventually gave me the pistol.

She said that she had awakened with a great deal of anxiety and found herself in the bathroom with the pistol pointed at her head. She could not recall making a decision to get the gun and point it at herself. She said that she was afraid that she was going to kill herself. She asked that I keep the gun for her protection. She was hospitalized for a while but never returned to class. I always wondered what happened to Angie.

Another incident at the school also gave me pause. Vivian (not her real name) was a tall and large African-American woman who was very pleasant to me. She was always polite and very complimentary of what she had learned. She loved to take spelling tests. One day she came in a little quiet. We were all used to joking with one another and could always rely on her to make us laugh. Halfway through the day, she came apart. She began screaming and throwing tables and chairs around. She said that she was fed up with trying so hard but getting nowhere.

She was still enraged when she ran out and attempted to drive off in her old station wagon. As the car began moving, I talked to her through her car window. I was afraid that she would get in a wreck if I let her go like that. She eventually stopped, cried a lot, but calmed down. She probably had anxiety issues and perhaps had not taken her medication. It was a frightening moment, as I knew I would not have been able to physically restrain her if she had started fighting with me or the other students. This very confident self-assured woman was now a wounded human being who was expressing so much pain and need.

She was disenrolled from the class by her counselor, and although she returned to class weeks later, she was never the same. I believe that they prescribed a heavier dosage of medicine, as she seemed sedated most of the time and lost interest in school.

The adventures at DVR came to an end when a tornado literally blew into town and completely demolished the building that served as the school. It was on May 11, 1970, when this bad boy came into town. It destroyed one of the Chicano barrios, the country club area, and the gentrified area where my school had been located. The tornado killed thirty-three people. I was forced to accept employment elsewhere.

I soon heard of another position that would be opening up and that I felt was just down my alley. The organization was called Texans for the Educational Advancement of Mexican-Americans. Their funding came from the Emergency School Assistance Act, a piece of legislation that came into being as a result of Dr. Martin Luther King, Jr's civil rights campaign.

¿CUÁNTAS PÍSCAS?

The position called for someone who would coordinate educational information and services to barrio parents in three different school districts. This was at the time of much racial unrest due to inequities and discrimination in the Texas school districts. There were no Hispanic teachers, and the Hispanic kids were not encouraged to participate in sports or other activities that could serve to encourage them to stay in school. Many of the children were dropping out way before they reached high school.

For example, there were some school districts where the majority of the kids in the elementary schools were Hispanic. When they reached junior high, about half of that group did not return to school. By the time they reached high school, there was only a handful of students left. The most that graduated were one or two, if any. The parents of these Mexican-American kids felt powerless to help their sons and daughters and just became complacent in their attitudes.

I did get this job and my area was quite large, so I did a great deal of traveling. I organized councils, which we called *consejos,* in three different school districts: Amarillo, Brownfield, and Lamesa. From the north to the south, the distance was 150 miles. I lived in Lubbock, which was geographically in the middle of the service area. The consejos were made up of parents as well as their student children. It was for the purpose of discussing the Hispanic students' educational needs and problems and ways of bringing these to the attention of the school administration and/or the school boards.

We got the parents more involved, so they began supporting their kids like never before. It was very difficult working with the schools, as they were the most resistant to change. We realized early on that friendly talks were not going to work, so we looked for opportunities to confront these schools.

In Brownfield, an occasion presented itself when a Hispanic student was killed in an accident. The Hispanic kids, as is the cultural custom, wanted to attend their friend's funeral. The administration decided not to let them out of school to go to the funeral. One of our kids, who was wearing a Levi jacket with an Aztec Eagle on the back, got a broom to use as a pole and used his jacket as a flag and encouraged others to walk out. At that time, the Aztec eagle was used as the symbol for *la Causa*. The kids walked out despite the threat of getting expelled from school.

We convened the consejo and compiled some demands that would be presented to the school. The demands were pretty simple but meant a lot to the students. First of all, they wanted to be allowed to return to school without repercussions. Secondly, they wanted an apology from the school for being so insensitive to their need to grieve their friend and classmate. Because they had no authority figures in the school, they wanted the school to hire Hispanic teachers and counselors who could better understand their issues and who would provide encouragement for them to continue in school. We got most of the demands, with the school promising to recruit more Hispanic teachers. For this we just had to wait and see.

In Lamesa, we were presented with a similar situation, and the Chicano students walked out. We met at the Catholic Church, which seemed sympathetic to the plight of the Hispanic students. The night of the meeting, the police were everywhere around the church. Any outsider driving into town was given an escort by the police, myself included. They were afraid of a riot, as this school was a lot larger than the one in Brownfield. After several of us got up and talked to the students and parents present, we explained that we were prepared to write out the demands the kids had already been articulating regarding what they wanted from the school system.

The local priest then told everyone that he appreciated how everyone felt but suggested that it wasn't the time for this kind of action. He encouraged everyone to go home. We lost several months of momentum when everyone went home, because this priest, as they often do, carried a lot of weight with the Hispanic community. It is my feeling that the local authorities got to the priest and solicited his help because they feared a riot.

As was often the case in those days with good programs, the money for this activity was cut off before we could achieve full success. The program went under, and I found myself looking for another job. By this time, I was in graduate school. One of my professors told me that poverty –fighting organizations were looking for Hispanics to fill jobs in Washington, D.C. By coincidence I went to a barbeque and ran into a former Texas Tech classmate of mine who was now working in Washington D.C., Lenin Juarez told me of a job with his organization in the District.

I talked it over with my family and was mulling over this decision. My father was very old by now, and I thought moving over a thousand miles away would not provide me much flexibility if he should get sick. (My father later died in 1980 after I had returned to the Southwest and was working for the New Mexico State Housing Authority.)

My friend Lenin wasted no time in calling me when he got back to Washington, D.C. I saw this as an opportunity to see the East, the hub of where national government decisions are made. After serious consideration, I decided to accept the position. I would become the administrative assistant to one of the program directors.

I stayed with my friend Lenin Juarez and his wife Vera in their house until I had time to find an apartment for my family. I will never forget the day I arrived, and Lenin took me for a ride in the District. No matter how many times I had seen the White House on television and in pictures, I was truly amazed at the way I felt when I viewed it in person. It was like seeing a castle in a fairy story for the very first time. It was awesome!

I thought of my stint in Washington, D.C., as an opportunity similar to that of attending graduate school in a university in the East. I drove there from Lubbock to look for an apartment and to start my job. Enes and our son followed a few weeks later, after I had secured an apartment. The apartment was located in Alexandria, Virginia, and my office was at 1601 Connecticut Avenue in Washington, D.C.

The apartment complex where we lived was also the home of many other Hispanics working in the District. Some of them were from Texas and others from New Mexico. We soon made friends, and adjusting to the East was not as bad as was anticipated. We stayed in frequent contact with relatives and friends back home while we made new friends.

The District was an amazing city. You could feel the energy of the city as you walked or drove its streets. There was always so much going on, from frequent parties on the Hill to activities surrounding Congress and the White House. This was the time of the Watergate scandal that brought down President Nixon, so news stories inundated us with rumors of White House staff firings or resignations.

At first I spent a great deal of time in training, either at the office or at workshops or conferences. Soon I accompanied senior staff to the field and to assess housing needs or to provide direct technical assistance to organizations or communities. We had a travel agency that would book our air travel and a credit card that was used to rent cars once we got to our destinations.

The Housing Assistance Council (HAC) is a national organization dedicated to advocating for rural housing and developed to provide technical assistance and training to organizations and communities wishing to address their housing problems. HAC also had a revolving loan fund that we used to provide seed funds to these organizations and communities. It continues in this valuable capacity to this day.

Soon I was sent to different parts of the country on my own. I traveled from Pennsylvania to California and everywhere in between. I especially enjoyed the trips where I was able to work with migrant and seasonal farmworkers. I guess that I just identified more with them and wanted to do a special job because I understood their cause better than others. I had been a migrant and had lived in dilapidated housing and could identify with many of their experiences.

We had opened an office in Atlanta, Georgia, and another one near Sacramento, California. The director and the board soon began talking about a field office somewhere in the Southwest. I was still very connected to Lubbock, Texas, so my friend Lenin and I made a pitch that the office be located there. My hope was that eventually I could transfer back home. Because there was also a desire for HAC to work with Native Americans, Albuquerque was chosen as the site. Lenin had worked in Albuquerque before, so he did most of the leg work for the establishment of the office. I became the deputy director of the office until the director resigned, and I became the director. My region included New Mexico and four surrounding states.

Altogether I worked for HAC for seven years. I was then recruited by Governor Bruce King to direct the housing programs for New Mexico. I became the director of the New Mexico State Housing Authority, a position I held for four and one half years. I enjoyed this job immensely. It provided me an opportunity to travel throughout the state and to represent the state at regional and national events. During the legislative session, it was my duty to inform the legislature of the housing needs in the state and to advocate for more housing programs, especially for the elderly and the rural poor. I would testify at committees and subcommittees. I found the legislators quite receptive most of the time.

I remained in this position six months into the next Governor's tenure. I had campaigned for Governor Tony Anaya, who succeeded Governor King, and I really liked his progressive approach. However, I sensed that his appointed Secretary of the Economic and Development Department wanted to appoint his own person. Given that mine was an exempt position, I resigned. Roberto Mondragon, who had been Governor King's Lieutenant Governor, was appointed to the position.

I then joined a well-respected real estate firm in Los Lunas, New Mexico. I felt that my knowledge of housing programs would easily transfer to selling real estate. I had helped a Valencia County real estate broker, Gerald Chavez, to develop a twenty-eight unit rental project in Los Lunas. I also helped him convert an apartment complex into condominiums, which he later sold individually. Moreover, I was glad that he showed an interest in developing land and perhaps constructing houses. This was something I had always been interested in.

Shortly after learning real estate, I partnered with Mr. Chavez to start a field office in Albuquerque. This did not prove to be a positive venture. At this time I was also experiencing a great many domestic problems, including my wife having to be hospitalized for depression. With three children to consider, I starting looking for another job where I would not have to rely solely on commissions. I worked for Mr. Chavez as a salesman and as a business partner for almost three years.

Real estate turned out to be more of a challenge than I expected. My heart was just not into the business, especially when I was having so many problems at home. Also, a business venture did not materialize with its expected profit. I was forced to sell my piece of a general partnership in an apartment complex in the town of Bernalillo because I needed cash and so could not benefit from a tax write off.

My job search led me to the New Mexico State Library, where I looked up every job listing and tested for the jobs that were suitable to my educational background and work experience. With a master's degree, I applied for human service jobs. I even solicited the help of friends in politics. I was able to land a job with the Children, Youth and Families Department (CYFD). I began working in Rio Rancho in July 1987 as a beginning social worker. At first it was quite awkward, as the local management team felt that they did not have a choice in who was hired. Later, after I had proven myself, my supervisor, the regional manager and I, became very close friends and remain so to this day.

By beginning at an entry level position, I made a complete circle from where I had started. I was not used to starting at the bottom, as in recent jobs I had reached much higher levels. Nonetheless, I swallowed my pride and tackled my new job with a great deal of enthusiasm. It was a generic office, so I had duties as an investigator as well as a treatment worker. I also was called upon to participate in training foster parents. Foster parents were part of the treatment team whose goal was to work with the parents to make it possible to return their children to them. In many large offices, workers specialize and are assigned to work in only one area. In smaller offices, we had to work in all components of social work. I didn't need as much supervision as others because I had done this job before. The difference was the paper work, which was a great deal more than it had been when I was doing the job some twenty years before.

I really liked working in the Rio Rancho Child Protective Services (CPS) office because I had a good relationship with the workers there, and my supervisors were very supportive.

We worked very well with the schools and law enforcement, so we partnered in attacking the problems of abuse and neglect. I learned in my social work training that, we social workers could be effective change agents. The court would conclude that the families that we worked with needed to make sometimes drastic changes in order to effectively parent their young ones. Change is as hard for them as it is to most of us, and we saw them fighting change with a great deal of energy when trying to get their children back.

Several cases in Rio Rancho come to mind as particularly challenging. One will always remain in my memory. I was working with a family composed of a mom and a dad who were physically challenged. The mom was confined to her bed, and the dad had suffered a stroke and was physically impaired and unable to communicate in a clear manner. Their fifteen-year-old son, who I will call James, had been severely neglected, and the dad had threatened him physically.

James was a good-looking kid with long blond hair who had ambitions of being a rock star. James was having a great deal of problems in school, and the parents were at their wits' end as to how to deal with his behavior. Eventually he was placed in a group home and seemed to be responding to supervision. James committed an offense that brought him under the supervision of a criminal court. As such, he had to be supervised by the Juvenile Probation office and had to jump through some hoops for them. Both of our agencies teamed up to provide him with guidance in an effort to hopefully turn him around.

Interestingly enough, James was a very likeable kid. He was assessed as being depressed but otherwise seemed to be making much progress. However, one day he ran away from the facility. Goofing around, he and his friends made an enemy of a well-known adult bully. They did something to the bully, and he proceeded to chase James. He caught up with him and beat James up. James reacted by pulling a knife from his pocket and stabbing the man in the heart. He had been backed into a corner by this man who was almost twice his size. It was just a knee-jerk reaction, but the man died instantly. James ran away, and the police went looking for him.

Both CPS and the Juvenile authorities determined that if the man had not chased him, he would not have pulled his knife to defend himself. Given the seriousness of the charge, we were afraid that if the police found him and he resisted, they would surely shoot him. James called me from a pay phone, just wanting to talk to somebody. I could tell that he was scared and very confused. I talked to him about giving himself up, which he considered but was not ready to do.

He called again and this time we determined that he was at his parents' home. I kept him on the phone for a long time, going over his options, and while we were on the phone the police rushed in and took him down. I attended every court hearing until he entered an Alford plea. In essence he did not plead guilty but agreed to be sentenced as if he had been found guilty. I really believe that he could have turned his life around. Neglect by his parents and a strong will on his part led him to choose the wrong path.

Another case comes to mind. I was on call one weekend when I received word that an eighteen-month-old baby had been taken to the hospital with severe injuries. In CPS, a worker is on call to respond to this type of emergency twenty-four hours a day. I arrived at the hospital and went to see the child. He was a little Hispanic boy who was in a coma. I could not see a place on his body that did not have bruises. He was diagnosed with a subdural hematoma.

The mother was a Mexican national. She and her sister were at the hospital, having being dropped off by her husband who, I felt, did not want to be questioned about the bruises. I interviewed her, and she told me the same story she was telling the police. She said that the baby fell from the bed and hit his head on the floor.

The officer present had the good sense to call another officer in Rio Rancho and request that he go to the house and see if what she said made sense. She and her husband lived in a mobile home. The bed in question was some eighteen inches from the carpeted floor. The Rio Rancho Police were not buying the story, but their harshness in their communication with this woman, who could not speak English, made me feel a little sympathy toward her. The same night, to save the baby, the doctors had to operate on him to remove part of his brain.

The mother stuck to her story until early morning, when she confessed that she had thrown the baby against the wall, perhaps more than one time. Both the father and the mother of the baby were arrested.

I was called as a witness at the criminal trial that found them both guilty, the mother receiving the greatest penalty. She got fifteen years in prison. I still see little Jimmy (not his real name) at functions with his adoptive parents. He is a friendly teenager, but, unfortunately, with the mind of a four-year old.

Another case is vivid in my mind. We had received a report that a child had been beaten by his father, so was refusing to go home. I interviewed the father at my office, and during the course of the interview he seemed like a very concerned father who was at his wit's end with his son. He blamed the delinquent kids in school and their influence on his son. He was also blaming his wife, who he saw as being very permissive with the child. When he left, I felt like I had made a friend and was committed to helping him with his family, particularly with his troublesome son. I then proceeded to interview the boy.

I asked Manuel (not his real name) to meet me at a Lota Burger, a fast food place in Rio Rancho. I thought that he would be more comfortable there and would perhaps open up to me. Manuel was a tall, athletic-looking young man. In fact, he appeared big for his age. This fifteen-year-old boy began telling his story in bits and pieces.

They had come from El Paso and were just settling in Rio Rancho. He stated that when he was a little boy, he began witnessing his father beat up his mother. He always felt helpless to help his mother because when he tried to intervene, he would also get beaten. He told me that on more than one occasion the beatings were so severe that his mother would have to go to the hospital with broken bones and horrible bruises.

He got to the age where he vowed that when he was strong enough he was going to see to it that his father never beat his mother again. He said that the incident that brought his family's problem to

CYFD's attention was because he beat up his father! He said that he was reacting to his father's physical attack on his mother. He said that his physically confronting his father surprised his father. His father was so embarrassed to be beaten that he started blaming the son to authorities to deflect fault from him.

I believed Manuel and thus changed my whole treatment plan to reflect protection for the mother and treatment for both the teen and his dad. His father's sociopathic personality had me completely fooled. This was a domestic violence case contributing to abuse and neglect of a child.

I was soon promoted to the position of Adult and Child Protective Service Supervisor in the Valencia County office. The workload there was a great deal larger than that of the Sandoval office. The majority of cases were for neglect, although we did get quite a few that were not. Eventually, I moved to Los Lunas and bought a two bedroom adobe house on one third of an acre.

This house proved to be exceedingly therapeutic for me. Since it was an old adobe, I had a lot of fun being creative and adding many artistic amenities. For example, I built a nice adobe back porch with a beautiful waterfall. In the front of the house, I made a funky-looking studio with an enclosed adobe wall. On the wall, I embedded a large coyote and a cactus. I remember Apá telling me once that he knew how to make adobes and that one day he was going to show me how. I had a friend who had some experience in this area, and he showed me how to make and stack adobes to make a wall. I imagined Apá looking down and approving of my adobe making!

By this time I was divorced and living alone in the adobe. Enes had left New Mexico and moved to South Texas. Although I enjoyed living alone, I really missed my two girls. My son, who was now an adult, was working in Albuquerque. I saw him occasionally until he left for Los Angeles.

Working in Valencia County was totally different. The staff was less than friendly, as they had hoped one of their own would become the supervisor, even though none of them had applied for the position. I was challenged all the way, making it very difficult to supervise them. By attrition, they were all eventually replaced. Things got much better after that.

Working in this business, you seem to always encounter cases that are hard to forget. One time I was helping a worker investigate a suspected child sexual abuse case. The family in question had four children, two boys and two girls. There were rumors that a sixty-five year old man was spending a great deal of time with the children in the neighborhood. I interviewed this particular mom and asked whether she was concerned about the man.

She said that he came over to have coffee with her every morning and had not even made a pass at her. She thought he was harmless and, as a matter of fact, she told me that she used him as a baby-sitter when she and her husband wanted to go out. The neighbors, she stated, did the same. One of the kids had reported that he had taken them to a motel in the eastern part of the state some two hundred miles away. I asked her about this and she said he kept them for a couple of days but she was not aware that they had gone on a trip. She showed no concern.

The police were asked to investigate. However, they told us that they did not have enough to get a search warrant. Through a community organization that I chaired, the Valencia County Multidisciplinary Team, we were able to convince the District Attorney to intervene. A search warrant was issued, and the police found several items, including pictures, that linked this man to the sexual abuse of several children. When the police went to his house, he was dressed in women's clothing.

Among other things, the police found several pictures of children in the nude. They also found several souvenirs that he kept, including a diaper that was dated. Pedophiles are known to keep souvenirs of their abuse victims. He was booked and bound over for trial. Later we got several phone calls from adult women who had been abused by this man when they were young. Apparently he had been abusing children for some twenty years.

The perpetrator was also an ordained minister, although he had not been practicing at the time of arrest. I found two Bibles at his home. He pled guilty to some lesser charges and was sentenced to eighteen years in prison. In effect this was for life, given that he was already sixty-five years of age.

Another memorable case was that of a little Mexican girl who reported that she had been sexually molested by a teacher. Her parents were Mexican nationals, and it was not determined whether they were in this country legally. She alleged that it was not a regular teacher, but a substitute teacher who had molested her. The sheriff went to the school and provided the little girl with a photo array. She was able to identify the alleged perpetrator who was then arrested and booked into jail.

I conducted the forensic interview of the little girl, as she could only speak Spanish. This frightened young girl described the perpetrator, the environment, and the circumstances surrounding the abuse. I asked her how she felt after the abuse. She told me that she felt that the ground was a little closer to her than before. I took this to mean that she felt faint after the traumatic experience. I totally believed her testimony.

The District Attorney took this case to trial, and I was called as a witness. The trial ended in a hung jury. The defense attorney did not dispute that the girl had been molested. He merely stated that his client was not the perpetrator. The case was retried in another county, and I again had to testify.

The defense attorney was able to raise in the minds of the jurors a reasonable doubt that his client committed the offense. This five-year-old was put on the witness stand, and the defense attorney disputed her testimony. He asked her several questions about what her perpetrator looked like. At one point, he asked her whether the man had a mustache, and she said that he did. Of course, the defendant did not. He offered that as proof that it was not his client who had committed the act.

Mind you, this trial happened several months after the incident and it would have been hard for anyone to remember every detail, let alone a scared little girl testifying in front of her abuser. The jury found the defendant not guilty. This man quickly left New Mexico and went back home to New York. I was very disappointed that we were not able to convict him and I prayed that he would not victimized other innocent children. I later heard that he had committed suicide.

¿CUÁNTAS PÍSCAS?

Another case can only be described as bizarre. The local police gave us custody of a young girl who had been severely neglected and was being compromised by her mother. We placed this fourteen-year old in foster care while we attempted to work with the mother. The mother never cooperated with the treatment plan, but we never gave up trying to work with her.

The young girl, who I will call Rosie, ran away at least twice before she ran away again, and this time we did not have a clue as to her whereabouts. Months later I received a call from the District Attorney in Las Vegas, Nevada, where she had apparently been staying. Along with her brother and his friend, she had been arrested for murder. Her brother had befriended a wealthy man who let them stay at his house. After some weeks, the man attempted to kick them out, and her brother killed him. They buried him in the desert, but, were eventually found out. Rosie told the District Attorney that she was a ward of the state of New Mexico and to call me to confirm this. I had a long conversation with the Las Vegas District Attorney, who told me the situation Rosie found herself in.

She later testified against her brother, and he and his friend went to prison. Her brother vowed to kill her for ratting him out. She was allowed to return to New Mexico. By this time she had had a baby. A man of Italian descent was the father of the child but he made it clear that he was not interested in being part of her or her baby's life. She later had another child, and she moved to Truth or Consequences, New Mexico, a town north of Las Cruces in the extreme southern part of the state.

One morning her former foster parents came in to see me. They had with them two beautiful little kids that they said were Rosie's children. They reported that she had left the children with a baby-sitter, but had never returned for them. The baby-sitter knew that they were once her foster parents, so she contacted them when she did not hear from Rosie.

Rosie had last been seen with a man who was later arrested for killing several women in the Truth or Consequences area. It was speculated that he hid many bodies in nearby Elephant Butte Lake. This man was convicted on one count of murder, but before he could disclose information about the other victims he died in jail. Authorities suspect that Rosie was one of the serial killer's victims. The children were later returned to Rosie's mother, as she was the closest kin. Rosie was never heard from, and her body has never been found.

After a couple of years, I was promoted to the position of Family Preservation Supervisor (FPS). In this position, I supervised clinical social workers who went into the homes of clients, offering them intense counseling related to abuse or neglect issues. These same families would have faced court sanctions if they had declined the we were able to achieve some near-miraculous results. The attraction to parents was that they would not have to face court charges, and we also had gap monies that enabled us to help them pay a few of their bills. The dynamics of a crisis intervention model served to help parents turn their lives around and take a more active role in the lives of their children.

While I supervised a team of highly trained FPS clinicians, I also assigned myself to some of the families. I remember one in particular. I began working with a grandmother who was caring for several of her grandchildren because their parents were unable to do so for several reasons, including the fact that they were fighting drug addictions.

I really liked the grandmother, as she was trying her level best to help these kids stay straight. I found the two boys to be very courteous and respectful towards me. They seemed to enjoy the attention that they were getting from this program, as I tried to spend a lot of time with them. One boy, who I will call Carlos, was fifteen years old and his younger brother was a couple of years younger. We talked a lot about the drug environment and their feelings regarding their father's living in a drug rehabilitation facility. Both boys seemed genuinely interested in not following in their father or aunt's footsteps, as both dad and aunt were currently fighting drug addiction.

I remember one day taking them to Tomé Hill. This a place where many Valencia county residents take pilgrimages during Lent. Usually they go to *pagar una manda* (fulfill a promise), or to make promises to God or a saint, requesting a miracle. During the Easter weekend hundreds of people trek up the Hill, which is distinguished by three crosses at the top. Sometimes they walk for several miles to get to the hill. I took the boys because I had run out clinical activities to do with them. On top of the hill, you can see a big portion of the Rio Grande Valley. It is an awesome sight! When we started up the hill, Carlos started running as fast as he could. His brother and I were not as athletic, so we tried to catch up but could not. His action really surprised me. When we got to the top and we started talking, you could see a great deal of joy in his face. He said that when he grew up, he was going to build a house on top of a hill like that so he could see far in the distance. Being on top of the hill brought him a great deal of joy.

A few weeks later, I learned that Carlos was killed when the car he was driving ran off the road and into a ditch which was very near his grandmother's house. In fact, his grandmother told me that he had come by earlier in the night to see if his cousin wanted to go with him. His cousin was not at home, so she begged him to come in and get some sleep. He just smiled and walked out of the house. Later, she heard a big crash. When she went outside, she could hear him calling, "Nana, help me". When the police and the rescue personnel arrived, he had already died. He had been under the influence of drugs and was driving a stolen car.

His grandmother told me that he had been trying to call me because he wanted me to take him fishing. I never got the message, so we never went fishing. I sincerely believe that he wanted to turn his life around. I sensed that he wanted to experience some of the normal things that other kids experience. The deck was stacked against him, as everyone around him was doing drugs. Hard as he tried, this was his culture and, as it turned out, one he could not escape. I always wondered if I could have had more of an influence on him had I taken him fishing. I also wonder if I could have prevented his tragic death. A position held with two years I was promoted to County Office Manager, a position I held until November 2005 the date I retired. My area of responsibility was in Socorro, Sierra and northern Catron counties. These counties are located in the central and southern parts of New Mexico. The main office was located in Socorro, some sixty miles to the south of Los Lunas.

I remarried in 1995 to a teacher in the Belen School District. We both shared interests in community work and we met while we were both volunteers for a multidisciplinary team developed to staff difficult cases. Though my new office was in Socorro, my wife Diana and I elected to continue living in Los Lunas. She had been diagnosed with leukemia and we felt a need to be in an area where we could quickly get to a hospital if it became necessary. Los Lunas is just twenty minutes from the nearest hospital in Albuquerque.

My previous supervisor, County Office Manager Pam McKenzie, advised me before I took the position. She said that I would only have three major problems and they would be personnel, personnel, and personnel. I quickly saw how prophetic she had been. I had to find a supervisor and a social worker for the Truth or Consequences office. In Socorro, I had to find a placement worker. This worker's job was to recruit, train, and license foster parents, a big piece of our treatment effort.

Also, very shortly after arriving in Socorro, I had to intervene in a dispute between a worker and a supervisor. Eventually the supervisor got another job and the issue went away. I was then able to promote the senior social worker to the supervisor position. After I had my staff in place at both offices, I did not experience vacancies for about four years.

I really enjoyed being manager. I took advantage of opportunities to inform the public of our mission and how we were impacting their the number of investigations that we undertook, and I made sure that the community knew where we stood in relation to other counties. I made it a point to involve community leaders in the activities that we sponsored as an agency and to provide information to the community. Also, I attempted to participate in as many community-sponsored events as I could.

I believed that it was really important to cooperate and work with the community, as many times we were the brunt of criticism simply given the nature of our job. Some people would criticize us for imposing on people's lives and causing hardship by removing their children. Other times, people would criticize us for not acting quickly enough to protect children and/or vulnerable adults.

I believe that in my area of responsibility, the community felt that we were part of their team to combat child abuse and neglect. In fact, in both of my offices, we sponsored a Child Abuse Prevention event every April. We brought families together for a day of fun, with food, entertainment, and games. At the same time, community service agencies and CYFD set up booths informing families about resources they could use to support families with abuse or neglect issues.

I enjoyed soliciting and getting support from the mayors as well as from law enforcement. In Socorro Dr. Dan Lopez, the president of New Mexico Technical Institute was always very supportive of our efforts, including allowing us to use campus facilities for major events.

One of my duties was to provide relinquishment counseling to families who were prepared to choose this route rather than going to court to fight for their children. I enjoyed doing this counseling, and I considered this to be a very important part of my work. Families were counseled on their decision to relinquish their parental rights of their children. They usually came to the conclusion to relinquish because they were not successful in complying with court-ordered treatment plans. The alternative would be to go to court and, with the help of an attorney, try to convince the judge to return the children to them. The court usually ruled to terminate their parental rights.

The counseling was part of the Children's Code. This is the part of the statutes that authorize an agency to investigate child abuse and neglect. The purpose for the counseling was to make sure that the clients understood that they would not be able to ever have their children back and that there was a good chance that they would be adopted by another family. Some of the clients were sincerely remorseful that they had neglected or abused their children, and felt a lot of pain at the thought of giving up their children. Others, it seemed, had no feeling one way or the other. Their addictions and lifestyle overrode any thoughts of reuniting with their children.

I remember one client who relinquished her parental rights to three of her children. She was a young woman with an addictive personality. Had she been born in a stable and healthy home, she was once probably considered a beautiful woman. However, when I interviewed and counseled her, she looked very tired and a methamphetamine (meth) addiction had taken its toll on her body. She told me that she never expected to live as long as she had because of her lifestyle.

She described her addiction to me, saying, "You know how you feel when you get up in the morning and go about doing your job? I can only feel that way when I am under the influence of drugs. Normal to you is abnormal to me and being on meth is the only way that I can face the day." She went on to have two other children who also were removed because of severe neglect. She was in and out of treatment facilities but none seemed to have any positive effect on her. In fact, one facility kicked her out because they said she practiced witchcraft.

We talked philosophically about the reason that some people die at an early age and others do not. I said that maybe somebody upstairs has a plan for those to whom he continues to give chance after chance. She told me that she did not expect God to help her because she had done so many things against His will. For example, she said that when she needed but did not have any meth, she would pray to God for a fix. She did not believe that God would ever forgive her for this.

On another occasion, I was asked by the Santa Fe Child Protective Services (CPS) office to interview a young woman who was in the Sierra County jail. Apparently they had recently returned her children to her. They had been away from her for three years because of neglect due to her drug addiction. This was a young woman who I considered to be exceptionally beautiful with a very nice personality. Even in her jail garb, you could tell that she had a lot of class. She told me her story.

Apparently, she and her husband were coming back from Mexico with a load of drugs. This is why they were in the Sierra County jail. Mexico is just south of Truth or Consequences, and Interstate 25 is often used by drug dealers to bring drugs from Mexico. Interstate 25 passes through Albuquerque, then Santa Fe, and on up to Colorado. This couple was from Santa Fe. She told me that she was relieved that they got caught because she dreaded the thought of always hiding and trying to stay one step ahead of the law. She said that her father had spent ten years in prison in California for dealing in heroine. Her mother was a druggy and a prostitute and still running around in Santa Fe. She herself had been "busted" in Santa Fe and spent a great deal of time in jail before she was sent to a rehab center in California.

She said that she had been doing very well and even had a job at a Walmart store. She had re-established a relationship with her dad while in California. She was doing so well that she decided to come home and get her kids back. She said that she drove back to Santa Fe and was very happy until she started to drive into the area that was familiar to her. She told me that she got this awful feeling in her stomach and began to cry. She knew that she would not be able to resist the temptations of the drug culture she had left. She told me that half of her friends her age were dead, either of an overdose or because of the violence associated with the drug scene.

Nonetheless, she did get her children back and everyone was very proud of her. Everyone was proud except her husband, whom she had been separated from. He began contacting her about seeing the kids. Later, he wanted to take her out. She resisted for a long time, but she finally agreed to go out with him. He started sharing some drugs with her, and before she knew it, she was hooked again. This is when he got the idea of going south to Mexico and picking up drugs to sell.

I know that CPS took the children back. I don't know whether the amount of drugs that they found on her and her husband warranted her going to prison. There is no doubt in my mind that she loved her children and that she really wanted to turn her life around. She was a victim of her own family's neglect of her when she was a child and her husband's taking advantage of her good nature. Of course she was also a victim of the Santa Fe drug community, where many of her friends and relatives, I am sure, have a similar story to tell.

There were numerous families who made a profound impression on me. My desire to facilitate the healing of these families and the protection of their children was my reason for working in the human services field. For every family that came to our attention, there were dozens more that were, for whatever reason, never reported. I take my hat off to all of the dedicated social workers who work in this important field. I am especially thankful for the foster and adoptive parents and also for organizations, such as Boy's and Girl's Ranches and El Ranchito de Los Niños that are able to care for many of these neglected and abused children.

CHAPTER 10

End of a Challenging Career

In November 2005 I retired from public service after working thirty-four years in the human services field. I worked in the private sector for three years in between. I can honestly say that they served to provide me with personal growth and a more and better understanding of the world around me. The time I spent in the private sector provided an opportunity to get out of my comfort zone and test the waters of the business world. I learned many lessons about business but much more about myself. I found out that the business I was in was ruthless. The bottom line was profit and many times this was accomplished at the expense of good families and, sometimes, friends. Business was not a good fit for me.

Working in the human services field taught me a great deal about the needs of people, especially the poor and disadvantaged. I learned how some families can be helped and unfortunately, how some choose not to be helped. I enjoyed being able to be of service but always lamented the fact that there was even a need to intervene in people's lives, especially when abuse and neglect occurred. It wasn't long before I vicariously felt many of my clients' pain and emotional wounds as they faced their demons in the only way they knew. Early in my career I left Child Protective Services (CPS) for that reason, but years later I returned to it with a more realistic approach to treatment.

My decision to retire came after a great deal of thought and some hesitation. My position at the time of retirement was as a County Office Manager. In essence, I managed two offices in two and a half counties in the southern part of New Mexico. I had been working in this position for seven years. Prior to this I had been a social worker and a social worker supervisor in two different New Mexico counties. Altogether, I worked for the Children Youth and Families Department (CYFD) in New Mexico for 18 years. Previous to this, I had worked for the Department of Finance and Administration and as the Executive Director of the New Mexico State Housing Authority.

There were many reasons why I enjoyed working in the human services field. Firstly, I was involved in protecting children and vulnerable adults. These are two groups of people that many times are victims and are powerless against those who abuse them or take advantage of them in different ways. Secondly, I enjoyed my clients and the other service providers and professionals that I dealt with on a daily basis. In my position I dealt with the non-profit corporations that, many times provided counseling services to our clients, to the independent therapists who conducted psychological evaluations; and, to the courts, who determined what clients needed to do to get their children back. I immensely enjoyed shepherding dedicated social workers and supervisors who often needed empathetic attention and a shoulder to cry on when they were exposed to the atrocities that human beings impose on children and vulnerable adults. I personally attended four funerals for children that were on our caseload whose deaths were related to abuse or severe neglect.

While I had the pleasure of knowing many wonderful and dedicated social workers, unfortunately I also encountered some who expressed no genuine empathy and who perhaps could have benefited from working in a different profession. Many were so engrossed in their personal issues they had very little energy left to spend on their clients.

What was always unpleasant was the protective service system that seemed to always be changing, demanding more from the field while telling us that there was no help coming in the form of staffing or other support. When a plan was approved to add more staff, it would take months before we actually had a person in the field office to fill that slot.

When I tried to advocate for my offices by providing documentation for the need for additional staff, I would be told that other offices had it harder than my area and that everyone needed help. I interpreted this to mean that it didn't really matter how important our need was or our feelings about the need, we should just be grateful that we were not this other office that the manager thought was even needier. I am a diabetic, and at a visit to the doctor six weeks before my retirement, my doctor had advised me to take a less stressful job. I could not see any other state job as a social worker being less stressful.

Even though my wife and I had been talking about my retirement for a couple of months, my decision to retire came abruptly. At a regional County Office Manager meeting, it became apparent that the "cavalry was not coming to the rescue." We were all aware that the state had just learned of a huge surplus of money. I asked whether our higher-ups were going to request monies to help us to do our job more effectively. I was told not to expect that we would get help and that the social work profession never had been and never would be a priority. The regional manager said that those who could not adjust to this should probably seek another line of work.

I tendered my resignation right after this meeting. The regional manager was probably accurate in his assessment, however, I was disappointed that I did not get the encouragement deserving of the question I posed. I could not see myself continuing working under someone who espoused that attitude. Previous to this, I had worked under some very good supervisors. Because of mutual respect, I still maintain a very good relationship with each one of them.

I had not worked for the state as long as was needed for full retirement, but, because I had turned sixty-one years of age, I could retire with partial benefits. I did not know whether we could make it on a retirement income, but I knew that for my health and sanity, I had no other choice.

The year before, my wife had retired with a medical disability. She had undergone two years of chemotherapy for leukemia and had received a stem cell transplant. I thought retiring would provide us an opportunity to spend more time together and saw a chance to start a new chapter in life. For the last ten years, I had also enjoyed my status as an adjunct professor at the University of New Mexico Valencia campus. I love teaching and I had always looked at this as an opportunity to share my experiences and knowledge to the students in my classes. Also, since many of the students came from disadvantaged homes, I felt that my story could serve to encourage them to not give up on their dream to achieve an education and get a good job. I was hoping to expand the number of courses I taught once I retired from CYFD.

I also felt that perhaps I could write or develop my music. I play the guitar and sing and have performed in churches and at special events. I felt that I would now have more time to cultivate this particular gift. I wanted to start taking art lessons, as I have always admired people that could paint. I had always wondered whether anyone would show interest in my story. I also wanted to cultivate an old interest of mine and start writing poems again. I am happy to say that since my retirement, I have had the time to develop all of these interests. I have now been painting for a few years and I feel that my work is improving. My oil paintings can be found at the Belen Art League Gallery in Belen New, Mexico. The Gallery is located across from Judy Chicago's Gallery.

Also I have written a another book entitled; "El Mundo de Noé (Noe's World) -In Art and Poetry"

CHAPTER 11

Mi Familia (My Family)

Lara Family

It is an understatement to say that my mother and father were very special people. Their presence is still felt by their adult children today, and there isn't a week that goes by that we do not recall something that they did or said. My parents weren't the kind that would show emotions easily. For example, we were seldom hugged or told that we were loved. However, all we had to do is observe them and we knew that the family meant everything to them.

As I mentioned previously, even though there were many in the family, on our birthday Apá would always buy a case of cokes and a store-bought cake to celebrate. He made all of us feel that we were special. His recognition of our needs and feelings was uncanny. Apá knew how important it was for Danny and me to have bicycles when we arrived at an appropriate age. Even though he bought us used bicycles, he made sure we had them.

He also knew how important playing ball was, so we also got gloves. We didn't get the real nice, expensive Wilson gloves, but, instead, he went to the salvage store and bought us cheaper models made from pigskin. He bought the kind of gloves that he could afford. I guess if you were a good player, it didn't matter what glove you had. I don't remember ever complaining about the kind of glove or bike that I got. The gesture was simply appreciated, as I understood that he had limited resources.

Growing up, I do not remember a time when I didn't see my parents as old. By the time Connie, Danny, and I came along, my parents had practically relinquished most of their parenting duties to our older siblings. When I played in Little League, I always practiced my pitching before important games. One time I could not find anyone who was available to practice with me. Apá volunteered. Given that I saw him as very old, I was afraid to pitch the ball very hard for fear that I would hurt him. I always appreciated the extent that he would go to insure our success.

Apá was always the disciplinarian. I remember one time in Wisconsin when my father was working in a factory and would not be coming back until the end of the week. Some of the older kids in the camp convinced me to shoplift, as they were doing. I stole a comb and some perfume. There was no reason for picking those objects other than that they were easier to get. My mother found out about it and was very angry. She told me that she was going to wait until my father came and let him discipline me. After four days mother told him what I had done, he just gave me a stern lecture and made me promise never to steal again. I promised him that I wouldn't, and I never broke my promise!

It wasn't all work for us. On at least two occasions, Apá took the family to the Breckenridge Park and Zoo in San Antonio, Texas. I remember that the first time that we went, there was a strong smell when we went to the monkey cage. Upon returning to Lubbock and while working in the fields, I asked my brothers and sisters why it smelled so much like monkeys. At first they couldn't figure out what I was talking about. I told them that when we went to see the monkeys in San Antonio that was what I smelled. They then started laughing at me because they too remembered that there was a smell of skunk when we were there. They told me that I had smelled a skunk and not a monkey!

Amá and Apá were very hard workers, and they passed this virtue on to each one of us. What we missed in socialization we made up for in the way we approached employment challenges. We also learned from our parents, through their modeling, to trust the Lord, have respect for other people, and have a good attitude about life.

I don't remember my parents ever yelling at each other or raising their voice at us in a disrespectful way. I do remember that we would never, even as we got older and moved away from home, ever leave the house without Amá blessing us. She would always say, *"Que Dios te bendiga."* (May God bless you.) I always appreciated those words then, and to this day I feel that those prayers have kept me from harm's way many a time.

Today, I find it almost my duty to also bless my friends and colleagues when I say goodbye to them. I have done it for so long that many of them remind me when I forget. In my practice as a social worker, I always asked for God's blessing on the clients I happened to be working with at the moment. Sometimes their burden was so overwhelming that only an intervention from above could help them. Of course, they would never know that I had prayed for their healing. I could tell the difference, as it was rare that they did not respond in a positive manner. I have always had a great deal of faith that people can change.

My mother would very softly hum or sing choruses of songs all day long. We called them *coritos*. In the mornings, we would wake up to her singing and her clapping as she made fresh tortillas. The clapping sound was made when she exchanged a tortilla from one hand to the other in an effort to stretch the dough to make them round.

Around the Christmas holidays, my mother would organize all of us to make tamales. The smell of the meat cooking and the corn *masa* (dough) was enough to drive you crazy in anticipation. My job was to *embarrar*, to spread the masa on the corn husk. My older sisters would put the cooked meat into the prepared masa. The smell and taste of fresh tamales during the holidays was one of my greatest joys.

Also, and usually on New Year's Eve, my mother would make a big stack of *buñuelos*. Buñuelos were made out of flour and sugar; they were round and bigger than tortillas. They would be fried in hot oil and got pretty crispy. They were sprinkled with sugar and a little cinnamon. Usually she made us hot chocolate to go with them. When the New Year arrived, Apá would go outside to see which way the wind was blowing. He believed that if it came from the east, it meant we were going to have a good year. The holidays at the Lara home were always very special.

My parents never talked about money or money problems. As a kid, however, I could sense when our money situation was critical. I would always hear Amá sing, *"Dios cuida de las aves, cuidara tambien de mi."* (God takes care of the birds in the wild, He will also take care of me) Somehow, it was her way of saying that we had to have faith that things would get better. And they always did.

I remember one time as a child, I was picking cotton. I felt sick, so Apá told me to go home. I went home, and Amá was alone. She gave me a Dr. Pepper and a slice of white bread with cheese. I felt so special and so loved. We seldom had white bread or soft drinks so it was a treat when we got them.

Another time, when I had just gotten a BB gun, I proceeded to test my skills in shooting. I announced to my mother that I had shot thirteen birds. Instead of being happy, she seemed disappointed and told me that one shouldn't kill anything unless we are going to eat it. I then dressed the birds, made a little fire, and cooked them. I took a little taste and almost threw up. Somehow eating sparrows wasn't like eating chicken! I have not killed another bird since.

After we moved to our own house in West Texas, one day my mother was alone at home. She said that a stranger came by and asked if she had a dime, which she had. He then had her place it on the palm of her hand. He looked at it and told her that she was a good person and her sons and daughters were going to do well in life. He also told her that there were many people who were jealous of our family, but not to worry about this, as things were going to be all right. To this day, every time I am feeling a little low or experiencing a problem, I seem to always find a dime. I feel very good when this happens because I sense that perhaps my mother is thinking about me and reminding me that things will work out all right. For me it was dimes from Heaven rather than pennies from Heaven!

My mother never worked outside the home. Her role was to cook and wash clothes for all of us who did work in the fields or wherever we found work. Also, she was the healer in the family. When any one of us got sick she knew exactly what to do, and, when she could not create the healing herself, she would make the decision for us to see the doctor. This was very rare, however, as she was very good at doctoring.

Her medicines of choice were mentholatum and rubbing alcohol. Also, she used *yerbitas* (herbs) such as *manzanilla* (chamomile), *yerba buena* (mint), or *estafiate* (wormwood) for stomach aches. The mentholatum and alcohol were used for deep chest colds. When we had unexplained *dolores* (pain) on our arms and legs, she would make a concoction of whiskey and moth balls. She called this *alcanfor*. It worked every time, especially when she combined this with prayer. She always bought us oranges to eat, especially in the winter. For a little indigestion, when available, sometimes we were given a 7-Up. She had an instinct for knowing what to do.

I guess I have always been afraid of lightening storms. When the storms came when I was a child, sometimes we would see a neighbor woman go to the front porch and place a large butcher knife in a small child's hand, point the knife toward the cloud, and make the sign of the cross. She said this would cut the power of the storm. My mother would always cover the windows and the mirrors in the house, as she believed that the lightning could be reflected from those objects toward us.

Amá was indeed a special person. One time, when she and Apá came to see me in Albuquerque where I lived, I took them to the flea market at the Albuquerque fairgrounds. While we were walking down the aisles looking for treasures, a Native American woman stopped Amá. She didn't say anything, but placed a beaded necklace on her and then walked away. We don't know who this beautiful old woman was, but she certainly recognized something in my mother. They seemed to connect at some spiritual level.

When I am asked to talk about my brothers and sisters, I always do with great enthusiasm and joy. Every time I think about them, I remember something special about each one, and I jump at the chance to share it with others.

Pablo (Paul) was the first-born in our family. It was a joy to be around my brother Paul. He was married about the time that I was born, so I have no recollection of how he interacted within our nuclear family then. I have heard some wonderful stories. I do remember that, as a married man, he was a good person. He was always considerate of every one of us and he always had a warm smile for each of us. He would take us kids to the movies and to the drive-in. His son Augie and I were very close, so either Augie would spend overnights at our house or I would stay at his.

I loved to stay over at Paul's house because they had a little more money than we did, so they always had good food, including ice cream. He also would give us rides on the tractor and did his share of teaching us how to work. Paul did not attend church, but I remember that every Sunday he would take out his Bible and read aloud for at least thirty minutes. This was his way of worshipping on Sunday.

¿CUÁNTAS PÍSCAS?

I remember one time that Augie and I were helping Paul irrigate. Someone had killed a skunk and it was right in the middle of the field, smelling up the world. Paul told us that skunk and other animal pelts were valuable, as people would buy them to make coats and other clothing. When he left for a couple of hours, Augie and I thought we would make a little money. We pulled that skunk all the way to the end of the rows so we could skin it and sell the pelt. When Paul came back and we told him what we had done, he laughed at us and explained that it wasn't that easy to go into business. Now we smelled like nobody's business!

Amá

June 23, 2006

"Esa señora preciosa, esposa de don David. *Siempre le gustava sentarse en el portal de enfrente. Siempre acompañada de su perrita, esperando la visita de sus hijos, con ningun deseo de salir.*"

She was mother to 12 children
but she was *"Ama"* to dozens more.
Relatives, friends and even strangers,
were blessed as they walked out the door

She loved the flowers and the trees,
she loved to see things grow.
She would offer you food for your body
and always a prayer for your soul.

When she still had her health,
and cooked meals for the clan,
she would do so praying softly,
for the crops and for the land.

¿CUÁNTAS PÍSCAS?

She would sing songs of praise
and many of thanksgiving.
She would offer prayers for all of us,
for our friends and for the needy.

Always when hard times came, she would sing and she would pray.
With confidence she would tell us,
We will see a better day.

She loved to laugh
and share humorous stories.
And Amá always had a way,
To make you forget your worries.

I am blessed because I knew her,
as a son and as a friend.
And many of the things she tried to teach me,
I am just beginning to understand.

Paul had volunteered for the Civilian Conservation Corp (CCC) when he was seventeen. The CCC was a government program to help unemployed young men during the Great depression. In the CCC, he learned to read as well as the value of dressing up nicely. He always had a lot of class when it came to the selection of his wardrobe. Paul was the kind of man who could always be counted on to help those in need. Also, I never heard of anyone who ever said anything bad about him. He liked to joke a lot and in his later years, he was fond of reminiscing with my brother David who he called "mi carnal", about living and working at Kennedy Ranch or about the many trips that the family took to Wisconsin. (Carnal is a slang word meaning brother. It is used with wanting to imply affection toward your blood brothers or your very close male friends.)

Paul and his wife Lourdes suffered a great tragedy when they lost their young son, Paul Junior. Junior was killed by a drunk driver when Junior was pulling out of a gas station. He was only eighteen years old and his senseless death affected all of us. This was the first death in the family that I had ever experienced.

Paul was a diabetic and spent the last few years before his death in dialysis. I remember his last words to me when I visited him in the hospital as he was dying. He told me, "You've come a long way." I was never sure if he meant that I had traveled a long distance or that I had accomplished a lot in my life. I'd like to think he meant the latter.

I never really got to know my sister Isidra, who we called Chila. She was married when I was very young, and I only knew her because my parents visited her family often. She and her husband Julian, lived in Caldwell, Texas, about 50 miles from Thrall where we lived. When we moved to Lubbock, they would come to visit us there.

Chila was very pretty and was always very kind and considerate. When my mother was in her older years, Chila would come and stay at our home for several weeks just to be with Amá and to help out. She reared some very fine sons and daughters. She had three daughters and four sons. She died of cancer some years ago. Her sons and daughters talk about her like we talk about Amá, with a great deal of respect, joy, and love. She was an avid gardener and she liked to sing. She was a Christian woman who loved her family dearly and sacrificed for them without complaint. It made you feel good to be around her.

Marta also married when I was quite young, so I don't remember much about the time when she lived with us. I do remember her as a married woman. Marta had been socialized a little differently from my other sisters. She learned to drive and sometimes had jobs working in stores or places away from the fields. She was very assertive and always seemed sure of herself.

Marta seemed to appreciate education to the point that she always helped my mother when special projects came along for us kids. She bought my graduation ring when I graduated from high school, as well as my college ring later. She enjoyed a very stable marriage and reared a very nice family. She had three daughters and one son.

Marta always lived near my parents so was available to help out in family emergencies or whenever she was needed. I remember when my car didn't start a couple of times and I needed to get to my classes at Texas Tech. It was Marta who got in her car and took me to campus.

As were the rest of my sisters, Marta was a very good-looking woman during her younger years. Like Paul, Marta was a diabetic, and spent her last few years in dialysis. She eventually died of heart complications related to the diabetes.

Ester is another of my seven sisters. She lived with us most of the time I was growing up. She worked in the fields and was an exceptionally good cotton picker. She liked to bake and on occasions she would make us a banana pudding that was out of this world. As we were a very large family, she would carefully give us portions so that everyone of us would get a piece. Sometimes these pieces were, in my opinion, very, very small. Maybe that's why I learned to appreciate banana pudding to the degree that I do today.

Ester has a great sense of humor and a wonderful memory. She is the oldest in the family now and has kept the history of the family in her mind. She can always be called upon when someone does not remember some happening in our youth. She also has a large collection of old family pictures. She has two daughters, one son, and several grandchildren. She and her husband have always lived on a farm. Ester has a great deal of faith in healing, and she has always been a little more sensitive than any of our siblings.

Next in line is my brother David. David quit school when he was in the third grade, and he always regretted having done so. He always bought the newspaper and subscribed to magazines such as *Life* so he could be well informed about what was going on in the world. He also was the one who would always lend Danny and me his car when we had important events in college. It wasn't unusual for him to slip us a couple of bucks when we were a little low on cash. David was a natural born musician that played the accordion and the guitar. Before his death, he was getting pretty good at also playing the piano. He enjoyed a great marriage and while staying very close to his brothers and sisters whom he called weekly. David's gift was his loyalty to his family and his desire to always stay in touch with his siblings. When I was a young teen, I would spend a lot of time with him irrigating cotton. He was always patient and a hard worker. One thing, however. He never worked on Sunday. I do not remember him ever going to church, so he wasn't religious. However, he did not feel that people should work on Sundays.

David was a laborer and one time got a job in the construction of a small theme park for children called Tiny Texan. All of the laborers, who were Hispanics, were very proud of their work and talked about how nice the park was going to be when they could take their own children there. They were all notified, however, that the park was for Whites only, and that they would not be able to bring their families. Everyone joined my brother David in walking off the job in protest. This was no small gesture as good jobs were hard to find at the time.

I remember when I had a financial set-back and I had no car, he gave me one that he was not using anymore. I had been working in real estate and was having a difficult time at it. I will never forget that wonderful act of kindness which played a big role in my getting back on my feet. He enjoys a very kind wife and the love of his three adult children and several grandchildren. David is fond of telephoning every one of his brothers and sisters. He also calls aunts and uncles and then reports to each one of us how the others are doing. David's gift is his loyalty to his family and his dedication to always staying in touch with us.

While at his house one time, I once heard a man come by looking for David. The man said, *"Ando buscando a don Davíd "* (I am looking for *don* David). I was very proud to hear David being addressed like my father had been addressed when he was alive. In the Mexican culture, using the word *don* is a sign of deep respect, almost like a title you assign to royalty. David earned the respect and love of many people, especially those in his family.

Estévan was two years younger than David. Both were very close and when they were young they enjoyed swimming and hunting together at Kennedy Ranch. As single adults, they would go out together and always had each other's back. Although they themselves were not instigators, they would join their friends who went to dances and other places where fights were quite common. As an older gentlemen, they enjoy visiting with each other and laughing while they reminisce about their younger days. Estévan shared that he was heading in the wrong direction in life. He felt that he was letting down my parents and he was also letting God down. He experienced a Christian conversion and went on to become a Methodist minister. I think it was partly because of him that all of us began attending church regularly. Before his retirement, he had pastoral assignments in dozens of churches and as a result, has friends all over the state of Texas.

Estévan built a chapel on his family's ranch, which has become the center of our family religious activities and reunions. Before his death, he enjoyed the support of his three adult married children, who for many years lived on the ranch with him. He was fortunate to have a wonderful wife and companion until the day cancer took her life as well. All three of his children are faithful to the church. They married spouses who also share their faith.

Estévan was the spiritual anchor in our family for many years until his death. He was available to us as each one of us experienced dark days. He prayed for us and calmly reduced our anxiety about events that impacted our lives. He conducted the funeral services of everyone that has died in our family, including his own wife Lupe. Estévan also served in the Army for a brief time.

Abigail is two years younger than Estévan. She was really the one that shouldered the responsibilities for caring for Connie, Danny, and me. Likewise, when my parents got old she was always there to help care for them. She has a wonderful disposition and loves to laugh and sing. She's a wonderful cook and also loves to bake special things. She didn't have much education but was our champion in encouraging us to do well in school. She draws very well and enjoys writing poetry and songs. Abigail married but never had children. When we were young, she would be the one who played Santa Claus at Christmas. We all knew it was her that would place *bolsitas* (little bags) of fruit and candy for us at our pallets while we were sleeping. We never saw her do this, so there was still hope that perhaps there really was a Santa.

Juana, who was two years younger than Abigail, died at age forty-five from cancer. She was very loving to my parents and worked hard in the fields. As a teenager, she had a penchant for rock and roll music and for sports. I remember that she always knew who won the pennant and who was playing in the World Series. She loved to laugh and to be with her Amá and Apá and the rest of the family. I never heard her complain about anything, even though she had a hard life in her marriage. I wish I had taken the time to know her a little better. Like the rest of my older sisters, she had very little education. Also like the rest of my sisters, she was a hard worker with a wonderful sense of humor.

Elisabeth, or Chavela, as she is called, is two years older than me. She dropped out of the eighth grade, but she made excellent grades while attending school. I do believe that had she finished school and gone on to college, she would have far exceeded any of my accomplishments. She is very smart and a very nice person. She and her husband Joe had four daughters and one son. She and I used to sing in church when we were teenagers. She sings beautifully and has passed this on to her daughters. She enjoys participating in church and in tending to her grandchildren. She also loves the Lord and has found peace in His word.

Little Church in the Woods

Written by Noé Lara
February 2007

A labor of love indeed,
is this little church in the woods.
Inspired by his love for Jesus,
built where some trees once stood.

Nestled among wild flowers,
cactus, trees and stones.
He erected this beautiful chapel,
With his hands, his blood, his bones.

He invites his friends and neighbors,
and his family as well.
Come and hear the word of Jesus,
Come and sit with us a spell.

It was built with so much kindness,
So much love, and so much care.
He delights in praising Jesus,
describing treasures over there.

NOÉ LARA

Reverand Lara shares unselfishly,
his casita and his love.
He understands that all his blessings,
come directly from above.

What a wonderful gift to have,
a little chapel behind your home.
Where you can sing and worship Jesus,
always knowing you are never alone.

The little church in the woods,
stands tall among the trees.
It will be there forever,
for generations to see.

You are welcome to come by,
encouraged to come around.
Don't forget that when you enter,
you are walking on Holy ground.

¿CUÁNTAS PÍSCAS?

Daniel, or Danny, is my younger brother. Danny was always very talented in sports and was quite popular with the girls in high school. He is a born artist and now that he is retired, he has rediscovered his passion for art. Danny was exceptionally good at playing football, basketball, and baseball. He enjoyed the friendship of many of his classmates.

Danny started college at Texas Tech and was then drafted into the Army. He went to Vietnam but later returned to Texas Tech and got a bachelor's degree. He later went to San Antonio and earned his Master's degree in social work at Our Lady of the Lake College. He and his wife Cissy had a daughter who now teaches in the same school district where Danny and I attended school when we were children.

Danny has been the anchor and patriarch of the family. He lives next door to my sisters Connie and Abigail and has accepted as his duty to tend to their every need, as he promised Apá before he died. Danny to this day loves sports and cars. He has season tickets to the Texas Tech games and has a wide collection of cars that he is repairing as a hobby. He was a counselor for the Veterans Administration for 29 years until his retirement. He has helped many veterans, especially Vietnam veterans, with psychological issues relating to war.

Danny, because of his job experience and his wonderful personality, has enjoyed the respect and friendship of many people throughout Texas. He is also a born artist and now enjoys making pencil drawings and acrylic paintings of famous people and members of our family. Danny and I became very close when he went to Vietnam, writing to each other often. One day, I received a letter telling me that he had not heard from his fiancé. He had been going with an Anglo girl in high school and throughout his freshman year in college. They planned to marry upon his return. I called her mother to inquire about her, and she informed me that she was on her honeymoon. Apparently, while Danny was gone, she had reignited a spark with a former boyfriend and eventually married him. Writing and telling Danny about this was one of the hardest things that I had ever done. He eventually became accepting of this and rationalized that perhaps there were too many cultural differences between them and it probably would not have worked out.

We went through another traumatic experience together a few months later. I was married at the time and lived in Lubbock. I was visiting my parents at the farm. I remember that we had had a big snowstorm, and the ground was covered with beautiful white glistening snow. It was a bright sunny day and everyone was in a playful mood. My sister Elisabeth and her husband Joe were also visiting. Joe and I went to the grocery store to get a few things, and, by coincidence, someone was calling the store to inquire about the Lara family. Since the store owner knew us, he handed me the phone.

It was a colonel in the Army informing the family that Danny had been wounded. He had little information other than that Danny had been evacuated to a hospital in a friendly area nearby. He said that we would be receiving more information later. He randomly called the store because my parents still did not have a telephone.

The mood of the day changed quickly. The first person I told was Apá, who was sick in bed at the time. After telling him, we both cried. I was worried that he would have a heart attack, but, being the man that he was, he just got very quiet and laid there in bed.

I eventually learned that the wound was serious and that Danny had lost a limb. I became very depressed and I did not know how to tell my family. It was killing me inside, and my wife insisted that we go over to Marta's house and tell her first so she could tell the rest of the family. My wife knew that I would not be able to do this myself because of the emotion involved. I felt relieved when I had told Marta and my brother-in-law Felix, the extent of Danny's wounds. They were visibly shaken by the news. Later, Danny was flown to Brooks Hospital in San Antonio, Texas, where we took turns going to visit him while he was convalescing in an amputee ward.

My brother Danny suffered a lot in his young life. Since then, every time I feel sorry for myself I think of his sacrifice and quickly get myself together. He paid a dear price so that all of us can enjoy the freedoms and opportunities that we have.

Connie now lives in Amá's house where we grew up. Connie became registered nurse and until her retirement worked at a local hospital in the capacity of charge nurse in a cardiac ward. Connie worked at this hospital for 30 years. Connie chose not to marry, as she was left in charge of caring for our elderly parents. She is a very kind and considerate person who has helped many of us financially during anxious times. She makes sure that the elder brothers and sisters enjoy a good quality of life. Connie hosts all of the Thanksgiving and Christmas get-togethers for the family living in and around the Lubbock area. She is exceptionally bright and confident and as a caregiver.

Paul's son Augustine, or Augie as we call him, is really my nephew. However, he has always either lived close to us or lived with us, and he is considered like a brother. In fact, I call him my brother when I and while we were growing up he, Danny, and I spent a great deal of time together. Augie was once married and when he divorced, assumed custody of his beautiful daughter. Amanda is his whole life. Augie made a promise to his dying father and my brother Paul that he would take care of the family. He took care of his mother until she passed and now lives with his two younger sisters. Augie is very much like my brother Paul. People just feel very good being around him. He is very generous and also very lucky. He loves to play black jack and the slots. He also likes to attend ball games and concerts. He always makes sure that everyone is having a good time. He is a hard worker, and Apá dearly loved and appreciated him because of his character and the fact that he worked with his hands. He was very proud of Augie because of the work that he did, and I think he would have been more even proud of him now. Augie is now living a very comfortable life and reaping the benefits of his hard work and intelligent investments.

It is difficult to describe my family and to be fair to each as I point out their attributes and what each one of them means to me. I just thank God that I was born into this family and I am forever indebted to them for all they have done for me. It is more than I will ever be able to repay.

My children, Noe, Daniela and Elizabeth Ann

CHAPTER 12

Mis Hijos (My Children)

We named our first born Noé Domingo. Before Noé was born, we would refer to him as Napoleon. After his birth (September 24, 1967), many times we still called him that. I anticipated his birth with a great deal of anxiety and joy. Not ever having had a child, I really did not know how to feel, much less how to act. He was strong and healthy and that was what was important. At the age of 23, I very definitely did not feel like a responsible person at the time, but here I was given this opportunity to succeed as a father so that he himself would succeed in life. My own father made it look so easy, but I struggled because I was just not ready to be a father. I loved *mi hijito* (my son) very much and I really wanted to do right by him. We definitely provided for his needs as any responsible parents would do.

I remember when he was little I would always tell him a story before he went to bed. I didn't read to him, I just made up stories to tell him. When he got a little older, we would use pencil and pads and play a war game. We would each have to come up with secret weapons to defeat the other. I remember one time I came up with the idea that I would catapult skunks on his side of the war lines. We would get a kick out of the many ways we would try to outdo each other.

Noé loved to go visit his grandparents, Amá and Apá. On the way down he would always ask in Spanish, "*¿ya mero?*" He was asking whether we were almost there. When he anticipated that we were near, he would put his little hand out toward the destination, and he would not put it down until we arrived. Sometimes he would have to hold up his hand with the other but he would not put it down until we got there. Apá dearly loved Noecito, as he was fond of calling him. He was the first grandson born that he held in his arms. Looking back, I can see that I should have given Noé a little more of my time and should have been a better example to him.

Enes was pregnant with Noé when she and her mother were involved in a train wreck. My mother-in-law's car was totaled, and they were badly bruised. It was considered a miracle that they were not seriously hurt. When my son was born I always considered him a miracle child, having been saved for a purpose. I am very proud of him, as he has always been very intelligent and a hard worker. He is a born artist who has a big heart for those less privileged.

After graduating from high school with high honors, he attended the Colorado Institute of Art, where he also graduated with honors. Later, he got a degree at the University of New Mexico. Noé has traveled to Hawaii and to Turkey. After leaving Albuquerque he lived in Los Angeles, San Francisco, and Florida, and now resides in Austin, Texas. He is employed by the Austin Convention Center.

Daniela Augustina Lara was our second child. She was named after her uncles Danny and Augie. She was born eight years after Noé. Danielita, as I still call her, was born with Downs Syndrome. When she was born the doctor explained that this was a genetic disorder that causes mental retardation. He said that the conditions vary from mild to severe and that one in eight hundred infants are born with this disorder each year. We were fortunate that Danielita's disorder was not severe and that we were able to put in place an early intervention program that has better prepared her to enjoy a good quality of life.

Danielita has always been very much loved. Because we enrolled her in a special preschool at six weeks, she has been able to do many things not normally expected of Downs Syndrome children. At six weeks she was receiving physical, occupational and speech therapy and did so until she started public school. I was deep into my egotistical drive to succeed when she was born. I felt very guilty over her birth and felt that somehow it was my fault. I did not know what her mission was at the time, but I soon learned.

Daniela shares the same passion that I have for singing and music. One day I decided that we were going to write a song. She named the song "Japan". When I no longer lived with the family, I would call her and we would sing this song. When we went to holiday occasions such as Thanksgiving dinners, we would always sing "Japan". Everyone always enjoyed us doing that and, being the ham that she is, she loved doing it too.

Danielita, unlike most Downs Syndrome children, is not shy and has a great sense of humor. She loves to keep up with young singers and actors. As well, she has a passion for the Dallas Cowboys and does not miss watching a game. I remember one Thanksgiving Day when we were visiting my brother Estévan and his daughters in Bastrop, we were just about to eat. As was the custom, my brother Estévan was giving the Thanksgiving prayer. We had been watching the Dallas Cowboy game before this so my niece Sonia turned down the sound on the T.V. When the game was over and Dallas had lost the game, Danielita told me that she knew why Dallas had lost. I asked her why she thought they had lost. She said because while her Uncle was saying grace, she opened her eyes and was watching the game instead of listening to his prayer. I told her that God probably did not mind and that it was not the cause of their losing. Daniela is very creative and was born with an inability to find fault in anyone. She accepts you as you are without judging and somehow finds ways to make you feel good about yourself. Daniela went on to graduate from high school and went to Cosmetology school. She passed her license test in Texas and does nails and facials, which she loves to do.

After Daniela was born, Enes went into postpartum depression. Daniela's birth was difficult for her to accept. She eventually recovered and began dedicating her whole time to Daniela's education. I attribute how well Daniela has done to Enes.

Elizabeth Ann was our third and last child born. She is seven years younger than Danielita and almost fifteen years younger than Noé. She is a beautiful, petite young woman with dark brown eyes.

She has always had a lot of spirit and enjoys expressing herself with a great deal of passion. Daniela was quite elated when Elizabeth was born. She treated her like a little doll and cared for her with great tenderness. Elizabeth always found so much love from relatives and strangers alike.

Elizabeth Ann is very talented. She plays the guitar much better than I do, and she sings beautifully. When she was a little girl, she had strong feelings about what and when to do things. For example, when she was to be taken to a friend or relatives' birthday party, or her own, she would be grumpy and totally uncooperative. After a while, she would decide to enjoy the party and would return to her old self. She also loves Daniela, and they had a lot of fun together when they were young. Now she continues to be considerate of her and finds different ways of showing it.

Elizabeth earned both her teaching degree and a Masters in administration. She is employed as an administrator with the Santa Fe School District in Texas, City. She and her husband Benjamin Davis are enjoying their three children: Liam, Phoebe Grace, and little Maggie. We are fortunate that they visit us regularly here in New Mexico. Often we get together in Taos, New Mexico and around the Holiday season.

I am cognizant of the fact that I missed a great deal of the children's life because of the lifestyle that I lived when we were together and because of the divorce when they were young. I deeply regret this and can only hope that as adults, we can grow closer together and are able to communicate with each other in some meaningful way. I have some wonderful memories of them when they were young and we were all together. Also, they are in my thoughts and prayers every single day.

CHAPTER 13

My Second Marriage, 1995-present

Noe & Diana Honeymoon bound

After being separated from my first family for almost seven years, I found myself growing tired of being alone. I knew I had to be very careful about deciding to remarry because I did not want to make the same mistakes I made when I first married. I wanted to really be in love with the person I married, and I did not want to "blow it." In other words, I did not want to abuse a new relationship by neglecting my partner, or, even worse, not being faithful.

When I first married, I was not sure I wanted to get married, as I was very young and, afterwards, never really felt married. The people that I associated with were also not very committed to their marriages. To the male friends I associated with, marriage was just something that you eventually did, but you worked hard to get away with as much as possible while away from home. I wanted to blend in with my married friends and just did what they did. It wasn't that we did not love our wives, it was just the culture of the time. Enes and I hosted several parties and were invited to many others. There was a lot of drinking, and we soon fell into that lifestyle. I also did not want to repeat this as my views on drinking had changed drastically.

When I started dating again I was always very careful. I took my time to evaluate not only the person I was with, but also myself. I truly reflected on how I was feeling at the time that I was with a different woman. I remember one lady that I met in church. She was very pretty but very much into herself. On dates she would talk a lot about herself and did not seem interested in my life. Other women just drank too much or, for some reason or another, never lived up to my standards. I also thought that because I was a kinesthetic person, I would automatically feel it if I had met the right woman. I was fortunate in having some very nice ladies in my life, but I never felt a special connection. There were two women that I would have considered good candidates for marriage, but, for whatever reasons, it just wasn't in the cards.

Through my job with CYFD in Valencia County, I chaired a Community Multidisciplinary Team. This was a group of professionals who represented their agencies and who participated in staffing cases brought to the group by one of the agencies. We would then develop a treatment plan, each one of us committing to do a piece of the work. These were cases that were very difficult and that the original agency with the case was unable to solve by itself.

Diana was one of the members of the team. She was a good-looking woman and very stylish in the way she dressed. She was a special education teacher with responsibilities that included conducting individual educational plans for the special education children in her school.

Upon meeting her, I was immediately attracted to her but was disappointed to learn that she was married. We became good friends and, in my capacity as a CPS supervisor, I hired her to counsel some of the kids on our caseload. She was professional in the way she took on her responsibilities. We spent a lot of time discussing the kids and talking about other things. I later learned that she was separated from her husband and that she was getting a divorce. I then approached her to see if she wanted to go on a date.

On our dates we talked about some of the dreams we had and of our interests. She liked music and was happy that I played the guitar and sang. We found that we were members of other committees, so we would also see each other at those meetings. We found that we had much in common and that we truly enjoyed each other's company.

We fell in love and, shortly after, we moved in together. We took a trip to New York to visit her parents, and it was there that I proposed to her. I was attending a Lutheran church in Valencia County, and the Pastor agreed to conduct the marriage ceremony. I also asked my brother Estévan, who was living in Austin, Texas, to participate in the service. The ceremony was Lutheran and Methodist and was attended by many of my relatives and friends. Diana's parents, Howard and Frances Fronhapple came in from Buffalo, New York for the wedding. I remember telling my new father-in-law after the ceremony that I would take good care of his daughter. His response was, "No, you both will take care of each other." Somehow, it made me feel good that he said that.

We have now been married for twenty four years, and Diana has supported every decision that I have made about career and retirement. We both enjoy a spirit-driven life, and since we have retired we have both taken up art and enjoy this activity immensely. Diana was diagnosed with cancer in October 2001, and received treatment at the Albuquerque Cancer Center and in Bethesda, Maryland, at the National Institute of Health (NIH). Her younger brother donated stem cells which she received and which saved her life. The ordeal of her treatments brought us closer together. I believe that she had some doubts about my commitment to her, but the experience at NIH served to quell them.

We both did a great deal of growing up during this period. Before going to Bethesda, we went to church where most of the congregation knew about Diana's illness and the fact that she was going to participate in a protocol in an attempt to reverse what appeared to be the inevitable. While walking to take communion we both started crying. Many of our friends present also were crying and surrounded Diana, showing her comfort and support. Both of us were scared to death as we had been given her chances for success as less than fifty percent. Diana was probably not any different from other people facing what many times is a terminal illness. Her feelings came out in the form of anger and her mother and I sometimes received the brunt of her negative emotion. However, when the decision came to undergo the transplant, she was very brave. My faith in God served to keep me balanced and gave me the strength each day of waiting. It was emotionally draining and, yes, it did test my faith. I would see Diana losing her hair, losing weight, and most of the time being so uncomfortable and visibly irritated. I took a leave of absence from my job and stayed with her for a month while she was in the hospital in Bethesda. After the stem cell transplant, I got an apartment for her and her parents nearby, as she was required to stay another few weeks on an outpatient basis. This whole process was in December and when the Washington, D.C., area was experiencing very bad snow and ice storms. I stayed with her brother in West Virginia, which was exactly a hundred miles from the NIH Hospital. Making the trip to the hospital daily in the snow and in Washington, D.C., traffic was not an easy task. However, at the time I didn't have much time to think about that. All I knew was that Diana needed me to be there, and I was going to be there for her.

I came home to New Mexico, and we stayed in touch by phone until it was time for me to go for her. Since then I have accompanied her to every follow-up appointment at NIH where we continue to get good news about her recovery. Dr. Rick Childs and the staff at the hospital have been outstanding. We had the privilege of having dinner with Dr. Childs and his family at his home in December 2006. He shared with us how serious Diana's situation had been during her stay at the hospital before and after the stem cell transplant. I will forever be an advocate of stem cell research as I see its potential to save countless lives in the future. Also, I have renewed my faith in God who was the source of Diana's healing as many of our relatives and friends prayed constantly for her. Diana would be diagnosed with cancer two more times. The second time her treatment was a radical hysterectomy for uterus cancer. The third time she elected to be treated by a naturopath. Instead of chemo she relies on natural medicine.

Even though we come from different cultures, Diana and I have not found it difficult to enjoy life together. It has been interesting, however. When we first got married and I wanted her to see something, I would tell her in Spanish, "*mira*". For a long time, she thought that "*mira*" was a special Spanish nickname I had for her. She told her good friend Linda, who is Hispanic, about this, only to find out that *mira* means "look." Diana was very disappointed to find out that she had not been given a special nickname!

I admire Diana because she is very loyal to her friends and because she has a deep love for animals. Also, she loves to read, and, when we're reading the same books, we enjoy comparing notes on them. She has taken up art and has learned that she really has a natural artistic talent. She excels in painting with acrylics, making pottery. As well, she enjoys scratch art and reverse painting. Diana fought exceptionally hard to get well and be free from cancer. She continues to do so to this day.

Presently we enjoy a modest retirement and have had opportunities to do some traveling, which we both enjoy. In March 2000 we went to Spain at the invitation of a person who shared the same last name as mine, Lara. She was from Valencia, Spain, but resided in Albuquerque. I thought this would be a wonderful opportunity for both of us to experience visiting a European country.

Also, I was curious to visit Spain, where many of my ancestors originated. My Spanish friend, Dr. Carmen Lara, would tell me that the Laras in Spain were not *gente corriente*. In other words, the Laras were not common people, but came from a distinguished family.

In Madrid, we stayed in a very nice, modest hostel located in the center of the city and right across from the *Museo del Jamon*. (Ham Museum) This museum has enormous selections of the many types of Spanish hams, cured sausages, and cheeses. We also visited *El Museo del Prado*. This museum contains the world's largest collection of Spanish paintings, ranging from the 12th to the 19th centuries.

Grandson Liam (6) Baseball player

Diana

June 23, 2006

She marvels at the Bosque,
and the mountains in this place.
As she contemplates the Universe
and God's artistic grace.

The flowers oh so bountiful,
And the majestic mountains high.
The landscape with such reverence,
to include the cloudy sky.

How many times before today,
has she marveled at this scene?
A picture perfect landscape,
or just a special dream?

She wonders how the angels feel,
as they fly throughout this place.
It's sanctified in Holy,
from God's amazing grace.

The Universe provides us life,
and unselfishly it's beauty.
Diana stands and meditates,
she knows it is her duty.

Sometimes we get a second chance,
to make things right you see.
The Universe provides us hope,
And grace until eternity.

From Madrid, we took a train and traveled to Segovia. There we saw the famous aqueducts which were built by the Romans in the first century A.D. and were in use until the 19th century. In Segovia we also visited a castle, *Castillo de la Mota at Medina del Campo*. Then we traveled to Valencia to experience the *Fallas* celebration. Fallas are gigantic caricatures made from paper maché or wood. Each Valencia neighborhood participates by sponsoring a falla and coming up with a theme, each trying to outdo each other. The themes that they select usually attempt to poke fun at recent political or societal happenings in which they are in disagreement. Some of these fallas cost as much as $100,000 and may take up to one year to build. We were there one week and enjoyed seeing the development and burning of the fallas experiencing all of the celebrations in between.

Santa Fe, New Mexico, has a similar tradition, which is referred to as the burning of Zozobra. Like the fallas in Spain, the celebration centers around the ritual burning in effigy of Old Man Gloom to dispel the hardships and travails of the past year. The effigy is a giant animated wood and cloth marionette that waves its arms and growls furiously at the approach of its fate.

From Valencia, we went by train to Málaga. There we took tour buses and visited Sevilla and Granada. In Granada, we thoroughly enjoyed the Alhambra, whose architecture was designed to project paradise on earth. It was built by Muslim caliphs when the Nastrid Dynasty ruled Granada.

I experienced the Spanish people in many parts of Spain. I can honestly say that I did not identify with the people there. I would try to find people that looked or acted like me or some of my relatives. I could not! I enjoyed knowing about Spain and marveled at the beauty of the land and ancient architecture. I did not, however, feel that I belonged there. Since then we have traveled to Cancun, Hawaii, and Alaska. We also enjoy visiting nearby states of Texas, Colorado, and Arizona.

Diana and I have a great number of friends who support us, as we both live in states away from our relatives. These friends are almost like family. We are looking forward to many other trips, enjoying our shared interests, and to growing old together.

Granddaughters Phoebe (4) and Maggie (2)

CHAPTER 14

Spiritual Development

My first memory of a formal church education came when I was about six years old. My family attended a little Mexican Presbyterian church in Taylor, Texas. It is my understanding that my grandmother, my mother's mother, was Catholic, but that my mother and father were not. I grew up in a Protestant world, but the Hispanics I interacted with were mostly Catholics. My experiences growing up were influenced by the fact that we were Protestant. I believe that my Christian father would look for churches that had Spanish- speaking services and which provided opportunities to learn more of the written word of God.

At the little Presbyterian Church in Taylor I attended a Sunday school class suited for my age. Before I could enter the class room, I had to recite by memory a verse from the Bible. I would always recite the same one, *"Dios es Amor,"* which means "God is love. I came to understand what those words meant when I began my personal search for the meaning of life and experienced the role that religion played in my spiritual quest. After working hard all day, Apá would make time in the evenings to teach us verses from the Bible. My older sisters tell me that he also did this for them when they were growing up.

I was baptized in that same little church long before I understood what the ceremony meant. Growing up, I was led to understand that

¿CUÁNTAS PÍSCAS?

because I had been baptized I now had a chance to go to heaven. I didn't really know what this meant, but it was clear to me that good people went to heaven and bad people did not. I was always led to believe that the alternative (hell) was just, well, hell! I remember as a child that, like the rest of my brothers and sisters, we would always pray at night before we went to sleep. I would pray for those I loved, but I also pray for the devil. I had so much fear of him that I did not want to get him mad!

Growing up in my family was quite an experience. Although from the outside it might seem that I lived a simple life, it was actually very complicated. There were many expectations that, in my mind, were difficult to comply with. I felt that the adults in my life gave me many mixed messages. Although they were not Pentecostal, my parents espoused strong fundamentalist beliefs characteristic of that denomination. This made it very difficult to find and enjoy activities that were not considered sinful.

We were encouraged to go to church and not to use profanity, drink liquor, dance, or have sex outside of marriage. In fact, my sister Elisabeth and I laugh about it today. We were not allowed to cuss, but we could say *"cara de masa aguada,"* which means "soft dough face."

My parents admired the Pentecostals because they were known to heal the sick, receive the Holy Spirit, and speak in tongues. When I was a child and my mother was very sick, the Pentecostals came and prayed for her healing. Later, for a reason I did not understand, my father would sometimes take me to Pentecostal churches during the week-night services, even though we were not members there. I think that he wanted me to be a preacher someday. Also, we would all attend the revivals when a faith-healing minister came into town to perform healings. I saw many people speak in tongues, but I never witnessed a healing.

We did not get a television set until I was about thirteen years old. However, after we did, and they started televising Billy Graham revivals, we did not miss a one. I still remember George Beverly Shea singing in his wonderful baritone voice and Ethel Waters singing, "His Eye Is On the Sparrow." I remember Dr. Graham placing his right hand on the side of his face as he watched and listened to this beautiful African-American woman sing in her most precious rendition of the song.

Growing up, my life was riddled with anxiety about my failure to live up to my parents' expectations in regard to religion. Sin was a focus in our family, and we were often reminded of the many around us who were skating on thin ice. I remember one time coming from a party where I had had a wonderful time. It was a little late, but I found everyone awake. I was immediately informed that my nephew had just been taken to the hospital, suffering from appendicitis. Somehow, because I had been out having a wonderful time, I was made to feel that it was my fault.

I definitely was exposed to the Bible and to people's interpretations of it. I was always very proud to understand it. I even took a Bible course in college. Now I realize that I never understood it at all. I was just accepting others' interpretations. Since then, my understanding has evolved. Also, I have come to believe that God enlightens us about His intent when He thinks we are ready to understand it. It is like the old saying, "When the student is ready, the master will appear."

I say this because I am discovering secret gems in the Bible that I never knew existed. I don't believe that I was ready to understand them when I was young. Also, I have learned that many things that I had accepted as truths did not necessarily happen the way they were written. Now I feel totally at ease in not literally accepting everything in the Bible.

I pray constantly. As we were growing up, any time we were faced with a new and difficult situation or when we were traveling somewhere, we were taught to say; *"El nombre sea de Diosito,"* which means, "May it be in God's name." I always felt a peace in my heart and felt assured that God would keep us from harm's way. Also, we were taught to say the Lord's Prayer before we went to sleep. Of course, it was always said in Spanish.

I feel that I have grown more mature in my understanding of God and religion over the years. I have no problems in believing in a higher power because I feel the presence of someone with me at all times. I believe that heaven is a place within us and not a community in the sky. I believe this is what Jesus meant when He said, "The Kingdom of Heaven is within you." And as I learned in Sunday school as a child, I believe that God is love, so people's compassion and tenderness comes from God. Our personal acts of kindness are inspired by God.

I believe that Jesus is God, so I always pray in Jesus' name. I have no problem believing, however, that Jesus (God) might have manifested Himself as another person with another name to other people who were not brought up in a Christian culture. I do not believe that there is a place called hell. I do believe that hell is the miserable lives that we choose to live in these times and the atrocities humanity imposes one on the other.

I believe that we came from somewhere. I like to think about it as a giant ball of spiritual energy. A spark comes down, and a child is born. When the child dies in youth or a person dies in old age, he returns to this ball of energy. The process is thus repeated over and over. Spiritual beings in this spiritual world may possibly interact with each other and I am sure that they visit us mortals from time to time. For example, there does not a week go by that I don't dream of a loved one that has passed on. I think that when we are reminded of someone that we loved and that has passed on, it is they that are causing it to happen.

I believe that because there is a God, man is inherently good. Evil is born when we choose to separate ourselves from what is good (God). I believe that man is born with a thirst to find truth, to be happy, and to seek a different and better life.

I no longer believe in established religions. I do not agree with those who claim to have all of the answers but would ostracize people who do not go along with their doctrine or that are somehow different from them. I believe that many religions are designed to exclude some and embrace those that follow without question.

I believe in prayer, and I find much comfort in singing or listening to spiritual songs. I resent, however, those that want to tell me how to pray. I don't like teachers to tell me I should believe "just because." I think it is very arrogant and presumptuous of us to think that we know conclusively what is in God's mind. It is hard for me now to accept that if you are not baptized, you cannot enter the Kingdom of Heaven.

I believe that we should spend more energy in pointing out the good things that people do rather than the things they don't do. Negative criticism borders on emotional abuse of those you criticize. It isn't healthy for them or for you. I believe that one should be able to explore mysteries of divinity and that God wants us to ask questions about what man says God is all about. We should seek to find God in every living creature, human or animal. Joy in life can be magnified through our continued search for beauty and for truth. I know that I find much happiness in my aesthetic journey.

We have no right to judge others or to condemn ourselves for acts we don't fully understand. Religion, I believe, is a tool for us to use in our personal spiritual path. It need not be for everyone, however, and their choices of worship should be respected and treated as sacred. We should be careful, if we are to follow a religion, to not follow blindly and accept doctrines without question. At the very least, we should sometimes agree to disagree with the leaders of the churches that we attend.

I am comfortable in believing that God manifests Himself to us at the most personal level. I see God in a beautiful sunset or sunrise and in the stars at night. It is just a shame that we have filled the earth with so much artificial light and loud noise that many of us cannot hear or see these heavenly creations. I have also been able to see and hear God in sermons, in songs or poems, and especially in paintings. I personally see God in the warm and sparkling eyes of children and in the more subdued but tender eyes of our *viejitos*, our elderly. Sometimes I am overcome with emotion as I experience this.

Although I never saw visiting evangelical faith-healers perform miracles, I have witnessed several spirit-inspired healings, and I wholeheartedly believe in prayer. My wife Diana's recovery from cancer is but one example. Although her physical treatments were in good hospitals and by gifted doctors, I attribute her healing to all of the prayers that came from across the country for her. They came from my family and me, from her family, and from our closest friends. They also came from strangers who learned about her illness. God's intervention is a mystery, but I have learned never to question His intent and to accept that He has a plan.

Lying in bed near the time of her death, my mother once told me a story about my brother Estévan. She said that when he was a child he contracted pneumonia and was dying. All night she held him in her arms and kept praying for God to spare him. Her own mother, who lived with the family at the time, kept begging her to stop praying for him and let God take him. She said at one point she did tell her mother that she had done this, but she really had not. At daylight, everyone was surprised that he had lived. Everyone was surprised except my mother. Estévan grew up and became a gifted pastor who helped many people and was always with each member of the family when we experienced dark moments in our own lives. God indeed had a plan, and Estévan's healing indeed was a miracle.

I love to sing spiritual songs, and, sometimes when I am singing, the Holy Spirit takes me to a place far away. I feel that I am in the presence of God and talking to Him. This happens especially when I am alone or when I am singing and can feel the presence of someone in the audience who is personally touched by my music.

I remember once when I was living with Enes and the children, that I was so unhappy. Not because I didn't want to be there, but because I felt I didn't belong there. I loved my children very much but by that time, Enes and I were enjoying very few happy moments together. I sat in a black lounge chair that I had gotten for Father's Day a couple years before and began to meditate.

In the process, I suddenly felt the presence of something holy. My skin began to tingle, and I became light as a feather. It was a feeling that I will never forget and that I have not experienced since. It was just for a few brief moments, but it felt like hours. The aesthetic feelings that I experienced in those moments were ones of joy, compassion, wisdom, and peace. I knew then that if I could experience this in a few brief moments, I could again experience it later in life.

Both of my parents had a great deal of faith. My father used to say that his prayers only reached the ceiling of our house, but that my mother's prayers reached all the way to heaven. He was a humble man, and I know for a fact that he had a great deal of faith. He loved all his children and always provided well. At key moments, he would dispense gems of wisdom that helped carry us through during our dark times. He also had an optimistic expectation that his children would turn away from making youthful wrong choices and eventually settle down and become productive citizens. He was rewarded in that all of us did change our ways and became good citizens.

Each one of us has followed in our parents' footsteps, supporting each other and praying and caring for those less fortunate. Those of us who were fortunate enough to have gained a formal education chose fields where we could be of service. My brother Estévan became a minister in the Methodist church. He served as a Pastor in the Rio Grande District in Texas. He eventually retired after more than thirty years in the ministry. My brother Danny worked for 29 years as a counselor, helping hundreds of veterans with war-related psychological issues. My sister Connie, and until her retirement, was the head nurse in a cardiac ward at a local Hospital in Lubbock, Texas. She has been working in this capacity for 30 years. I, of course, have just retired after working for almost 40 years as a human service worker addressing the needs of families, children, and vulnerable adults.

All of these occupations required that we have a great deal of faith. We had to have faith that we could do the job and faith that those who were suffering and were in our sphere of influence would be healed. I have always considered those who do the kind of work that we did as healers.

My brother Estévan, while in his twenties, experienced a religious conversion and felt a calling to become a minister of God. We began attending a little Mexican Methodist Mission, *La Trinidad Iglesia Metodista*. Looking back, I can see that attending church filled a great many of my social needs. There were many young people, and I enjoyed the activities that the church provided. Also, my parents would approve of any activity that was related to the church. There were many other activities that they did not approve of. Although I did not always agree with them, I always respected and worked hard to comply with my parents' wishes.

The building that housed the congregation of the La Trinidad was a long narrow white wooden building with a pitched roof. It also had a little rectory in the back. As people came in, the men would sit to the right and the women to the left. The men would take off their hats, while the older women always had their heads covered.

After the church congregation acquired a larger building in another part of town, this church was abandoned. When we married, Enes and I lived in the house that had been previously occupied by the church's ministers. La Trinidad was located in the very heart of *el barrio de Guadalupe*, the oldest Chicano barrio in Lubbock.

I was taught to respect authority, whether it was in school or at work. Especially, I was taught to not question the Bible. Both my parents were students of the Bible, my father especially. I believe that my father's talking about the Bible while we were chopping cotton was one of his ways of teaching us about God. We always attended church, including Sunday school. We always sat down together to eat, and my father always requested a blessing for the meal. My father did not drink or smoke, and he always attended church. The literature that he read was pretty much the Bible or books about the Bible.

For a long time and, after I separated from Enes, I did not attend church. However, I always considered myself a Christian. Living in Los Lunas, I was encouraged to attend church by the Lutheran minister of a church near my house. I eventually became a member there. I served as the President of the Preschool for two years and as President of the Council for two terms.

I really enjoyed the Lutheran Church because I was exposed to a theology that encouraged us to question the Bible until we felt comfortable with it. I also felt free to interpret the Bible as I saw how it applied to me personally. I had always considered the Bible as sacred and, even though I wasn't buying it hook, line, and sinker, I was brought up never to question it. It was liberating to find another way of interpreting its meaning.

For a few years I attended an Episcopal church in Los Lunas, but returned to Valley Lutheran Church where my wife and I were married. I attend because my wife and I enjoy the pleasure of many friends who are also members. Also, there are some people there who I consider to be anointed with the Holy Spirit and who believe in the power of healing. The church provides me the opportunity to play my guitar and sing gospel hymns. I am, however, exceedingly reluctant to participate in the administration of church business, which many times causes us to forget the true mission of the church.

It is difficult to write about one's past, as the things that seemed so important at the time, for whatever reasons, don't seem as important today. I was reared in a family that was not socially conscious, so we were never involved in trying to right the wrongs of society or to change the world. I grew up believing in God and was told to trust and have faith because eventually things would work out. If we found life to be unfair, one might have to wait until Jesus returned to rectify things and to take those who were faithful. I strongly doubted, however, that I was among them. Not that I was a bad person, but it seemed like someone would always raise the bar beyond my reach. I grew to believe that somehow, I just wasn't deserving of the rewards of heaven.

I did fantasize that eventually I would be successful in life, although I had no idea what success looked like. My gift, I eventually surmised, was in the process and in the search for the gifts that would bring me success. If I did have a gift, I concluded, was in not being afraid to try things. I remember repeating a mantra that I believed would lead me to the identification of my gift: "The infinite intelligence of my subconscious mind reveals to me my true gift in life." I don't believe this quest will ever end as, in the past, God has always found a way of revealing to me things that had not been on my radar screen.

CHAPTER 15

Those That Made an Impact on My Life

Just as there were dozens of people who offered help as I was struggling to get an education, there were equally as many who attempted to discourage me. One time, as I was chopping cotton, a woman asked me how old I was. I told her that I was fifteen years old. She said, "I heard that you are still attending school." She then proceeded to tell me to quit school and get a job to help support my family. She added that I was too old to still be going to school. Her own son was about my age, and she liked the fact that he had a full-time job.

I've already talked about my experience with the guidance counselor at my high school. He literally discouraged me from seeking a higher education. Also, when I was working for the Division of Vocational Rehabilitation (DVR) in Texas, I informed a counselor acquaintance of mine that I had applied to graduate school. Since he was in the business of counseling people in the area of work and education, I thought he would be supportive. He told me that it seemed to him that they were making it too easy for people to attend college, and he felt that they had lowered the standards for minorities. Needless to say, I was very disappointed in him, as he was trying to negate my effort to get ahead in life. In those days, there were few Hispanics in Texas with an education, and, either because of ignorance on our part or downright racism, there were those who wanted to keep it that way.

There were dozens of individuals who played a role in my personal growth and in my academic and professional success. I have grown to believe that we are all born with an innate ability to succeed in life, but that all of us have a slightly different view of what it means to be successful.

In this country we are doubly blessed in that there are so many opportunities not available elsewhere. I cannot imagine what my life would have been like had I been born and reared in Mexico. I say this because there are so many people immigrating to this country from Mexico and other countries in search of a better way of life. In the Southwest, most of the immigrants come from Mexico, where life is hard. If you are a family man, you will do anything you can for your family, even if it means entering another country illegally. My own father entered the United States illegally when he was only eighteen years of age.

Apá was the greatest influence in my life because he modeled how to be a man. I never knew him to drink, to gamble, and to not be attentive to his family. He took his responsibilities as a protector, a provider, and as a spiritual leader seriously. My father once told me that when he was young he used to stutter. The man I grew to know and love did not stutter, but he said very few words. He didn't have to speak. Once he did, you hung on to every word because you just knew that what he had to say was important.

He loved to laugh and he loved to sing, although his voice was not nearly as beautiful as my mother's. He was a hard worker and instilled in us the value of work. He never really learned to speak English and never attended any school beyond the first grade in Mexico. However, he was able to gain the respect of many men who called him, *el jefe*, the boss.

When I was young, it was never our custom to have a Christmas tree. I suppose this was because there usually wasn't any place to put it. However, Apá never failed to buy me something for Christmas. I seem to remember that for several years, while I was very young, he would buy me a little toy gun for Christmas. It wasn't wrapped, but I always got a little cap gun for Christmas. When I was older I would get a BB gun and sometimes clothes, depending on the family's economic situation at the time.

When I was a teenager, and after we had moved to our own home, he built me a bookshelf with crude tools. I used to put my textbooks and other school-related items there. The bookshelf is still there today. It was a great feeling to know that as long as he was healthy we would always be provided for. In fact, when he could no longer be hired because of his age, he collected Social Security. Until we turned 18 and while we were still in school, Danny, Connie and I received a small check from the Social Security Administration to help us with school-related expenses. Even after retirement and when he was no longer able to work full-time, he was still providing for us!

He knew what it meant to me to have a car, so he bought me a 1958 Renault when I was a junior in high school. Driving down the road in this car made me feel like a stud. I really thought I was somebody! One day, as I was changing a tire outside of our home, he came over to see what I was doing. Just as the time that he approached, the jack slipped while I was under the car. He grabbed the bumper with both hands and held the car up until I was free. After I got out and secured the car, he walked away without saying a word, almost as if nothing had happened.

I thought this was no big deal, as the car was a compact and probably didn't weigh much. However, when I later tried to pick it up, I got goose bumps because I could not lift it. I thought because I was younger and, I thought, stronger I would be able to do this. I quickly surmised that what he had done had nothing to do with strength. This is what a father is capable of doing if he loves his son.

When I was young and began attending church in Lubbock, I was used to older and very conservative preachers who seemed to address themselves to the adult congregation. One year, a young energetic preacher was assigned to our church. Ben Zermeño was tall and athletic-looking. In his wisdom, he saw that not much attention had been given to the young people of the church. He began developing programs for us. Also, he took the time to listen to us and discover our needs. He used to play football, and he talked to us about the importance of sports. I remember that even after he left the ministry, he was still helping me find jobs and always told me of opportunities to further my education.

Some personal problems caused him to divorce his wife, who had been born in Mexico City. No one really knew what had happened in his family, but all of us knew that he would run into a string of bad luck from time to time. While working in Washington D.C., I learned that he had taken his own life by hanging. We speculated that he felt very bad that he was no longer with his family and that he had left the ministry.

Ben was the one who told me about the St. Johns Methodist Church Sunday School class and was with me the night that I was interviewed for my scholarship to attend Texas Tech. He always advocated for me and believed that I had the potential to succeed. I will forever be indebted to him, and if there is a heaven, I cannot see God refusing him entrance.

Dr. Roberto Pedraza was another individual who made a difference in my life. He was a Methodist minister who became our Pastor. I liked him because he had a doctorate degree, and he did not have a poverty mentality. At this time, I did not know of any Latinos with a doctorate. I had very few Latino role models who could directly influence my thinking regarding furthering my education. Also, I now know that a poverty mentality often keeps many minorities from striving for higher goals in life.

At La Trinidad we were used to accepting the leftovers from the much larger Anglo churches in the area. For example, at Christmas we would get a Christmas tree from one of these churches. Dr. Pedraza told us that we had enough people in the congregation with the means to buy our own tree. He said that this year we were going to do just that. This made an impression on me, because many times we don't see our own potential and rely on outside sources for things we are capable of doing ourselves.

Dr. Pedraza also became involved in the community. I remember when I started working for Headstart, he was on the advisory committee to the school system implementing this new program. He was one of the reasons that I was motivated to also participate in my community.

Headstart was one of the programs that came out of President Lyndon Johnson's Great Society. It helped disadvantaged children prepare for entering public school. It also made it a point to get the parents involved with the education and health needs of their children. This has proven to be vital in the educational success of many children, especially minority children.

Ben's Rope

Written By Noé Lara
March 20, 2007

Ben was not a man of means,
some say he wasn't wise
And that he was generous to a fault,
Perhaps was the beginning of his demise.

He never met a stranger,
and he never liked to cry.
He trusted just like Jesus,
who also didn't have to die.

He was tied to just one Master,
he seemed happy and never bored.
To be negative about life,
Was a luxury he could not afford.

What made him choose,
To leave this world,
This world he gave his all?

Was it those people
who took from him,
That drove him to this call?

¿CUÁNTAS PÍSCAS?

They say he was depressed,
And that he no longer cared.
They say he was fighting demons,
That came from everywhere.

They found him hanging in his room,
His head was turned just so.
His big-framed body struggled,
but his feet never touched the floor.

Ben was my mentor, he was my friend,
he meant so much to me,
I could have visited him more often,
But I unwisely let it be.

Ben had a rope around his neck,
Long before that dreadful day.
He was tied to guilt and shame,
That never went away.

Like Jesus hanging on the cross,
His suffering did not have to be.
He sacrificed his life for many,
I know he did for me.

Another person who influenced my thinking and who was instrumental in my getting an education was the president of the Sunday School class that sponsored my going to college. The evening that I went to his house wearing my oversized suit and feeling totally out of place was, nonetheless, a memorable one. I saw what someone could accomplish if he had an education-a beautiful big house with a swimming pool, a wonderful family, the ability to have a great vacation, and lots of friends. This was indeed the American Dream.

It wasn't so much this, however, that had the most long-lasting affect on me. Some months later, after I had already started college, this very fine individual went into his beautiful backyard and put a bullet in his head. At first I was totally confused, as there seemed to be no apparent reason for him to do this. Here I was struggling to get through college and at the beginning of my struggle to get out of poverty, and someone that I thought had everything took his life. I began to reflect that things aren't always what they seem, and perhaps there isn't a strong correlation between wealth and happiness. This was eye-opening for me, as I started seeing my family in a more positive light than before.

Mr. Charles Houston was another person who had an impact on my life. He and his wife Ruth attended our little church, La Trinidad. He volunteered to play the piano for us and did so for several years. He was a nice, gentle man who, along with his wife, would invite the young people to his house for ice cream socials. I think he wanted us to experience what *better* looked like. They had a great big house with a very nice yard. Mr. Houston taught math at Texas Tech. When I was in college and having problems with math, he tutored me and helped me to understand the lessons. He would always encourage me, and I sensed that he truly believed that I would make it some day.

Dr. Walter Cartwright was another person who influenced my success. He was the chairman of the Sociology Department at Texas Tech. He made sure that I took the right courses and always encouraged me not to give up. My sister Marta worked cleaning his family's house he got to know much about my family. I think because of this he took a special interest in me. He guided me through my master's thesis, counseling me along the way.

When I finished writing my thesis, I found an ad in the paper by someone claiming that they could type papers according to the dictates of the University. I hired this person, even providing her a book on how to type a Texas Tech paper. At this time, I lived in Albuquerque, New Mexico, so I had to trust that she would get it done right and on time. I submitted the document and was waiting to receive my degree in the mail. Instead, I received a call from Dr. Cartwright, who told me that the paper was not typed according to the University's standards and it would have to be retyped. This meant my registering again for another semester and finding another typist. I registered again, and Dr. Cartwright found a reliable typist for me. At the end of the semester I received my Masters Degree Diploma, of which I am very proud and which has opened many doors for me since.

My American Dream

Written by Noé Lara
August 2, 2007

Miracles are wonderful,
But don't come without some pain.
I was looking for an answer,
I was looking for some gain.

I grew up poor I grew up proud,
But I couldn't find my way.
I prayed at night with desperation,
But by day I worked as if there no salvation.

I finally found a chance to shine,
I found a place to grow.
I got a scholarship to Texas Tech,
But little did I know.

The man who made it possible,
The man who signed the bills.
He went into his back yard,
And for a moment, it was deathly still.

His gun was pointed at his head,
He pulled the trigger twice.
He left a wife and three small kids,
No longer breathing, no longer wise.

This gentle man was lucky,
on this cloudy and dreadful day.
Of the two bullets from his gun,
Only one found its way.

¿CUÁNTAS PÍSCAS?

It made no sense to me,
I thought he had it all.
The American dream he owned,
Ended with his fall.

I was shocked I was confused,
I couldn't sleep that night,
For the man that I looked up to,
Had given up the fight.

My dream of being like him,
Abandoned me that day.
I searched from answers from above,
But like all men, he was made of clay.

I thought I saw an angel,
In the midst of the surreal scene.
He was trying to tell me something,
Not where I was going ,
But where I had been.

I was reminded of my father,
And all of us like him,
We treasured life, this sacred gift,
Anything less would be obscene.

If God really existed,
In this precious land of the free,
Why did this man take his life,
Not considering his family or me.

It took awhile to understand,
This lesson from above.
Success is not measured by what you do,
Success is measured by how you love.

CHAPTER 16

Lessons Learned

There was a time when I was young and trapped in ignorance and poverty. There have been many times since then when I wouldn't have hesitated to call that freedom. The positions that I held after graduation and the type of work that I chose to do carried enormous responsibilities. I often longed for the simple life when I just relied on hard work and my faith to get me through.

I did not feel that I needed much, and, although not an abundance, there always seemed to be enough, including opportunities. Because of my shyness, I didn't make many friends. Growing up, I was exceedingly insecure, so I didn't try as many things as I should have. I was afraid, but I learned to never let it show. I was lonely, but I never let on. As it turned out, loneliness and I became very good friends all through childhood and most of my adult life.

Looking back, I can describe my disposition most of the time as melancholy. Sometimes it seemed that there was laughter all around me. However, when I allowed myself to laugh hard, I became sad to the point of becoming nauseated. I don't view this as a negative. In fact, I now appreciate it as a gift. I believe that the subjects I paint, the songs I sing, and some of the poems I write, are tempered with a touch of sadness. This makes them stronger and more meaningful to others.

Because I made good grades in school and because I behaved well most of the time, I was looked upon by my family as the one who would succeed in life. Because I was the first in my family to graduate from high school, I assumed a responsibility to be a model for my younger siblings and my nephews and nieces. This was an awesome responsibility, and I was not sure I was up for the challenge. When I got married, once again I was faced with another and more important responsibility. It was to be a model to my own children.

The day I graduated from high school, only my sister Marta came to the graduation ceremony. No one else, especially my parents, had ever experienced going to the school. That one time was the only time any adult went to the school on my behalf. After that, other family members joined the parents of the graduating students, and there have been many other young Laras who graduated since then.

I was, according to my family, destined to be great and to become a man in every sense of the word. There was a time in my life when I truly felt that I had failed at both. I came to believe that to be great meant that I would be happy, and, to be a man, meant that I had to earn dignity and respect. I tried very hard to achieve this, but I came to believe that I had the wrong goals and that I was programmed to think that I would always be unsuccessful. Also, I came to believe that I would never discover the secret of being happy. Still I pressed on, and a little voice kept telling me not to give up. It seemed that an angel was always guiding my path because when one door closed on me, another one would quickly open.

Unhappy as I always seemed to be, opportunities would present themselves. I began to rely on them happening with a great deal of confidence and some joy. Now I know that it was just plain faith. Sometimes I felt, however, that I was taking my good fortune for granted. Sometimes I wondered when this good fortune would end.

For a while I seemed to have overcome shortcomings and despair. Desperate and many times self-abused, I kept the rhythm of the times. I am presently suffering from the "good life" that I thought I was living as a young married man. There was way too much drinking, but fortunately, someone's prayers kept me from drug addictions or worse.

At that time, life, bitter or sweet, I proudly claimed as mine and only mine. Many times I was afraid and confused but a shaman to the max. I might not have felt happy or successful, but I knew how to perform! My luck and my wit merely postponed failure, as my spirit was wrong and I knew it. I started to believe that it was inevitable that I fall.

It was memories about past successes that kept me going in my next episode in life. I remember one time, after my marriage failed, and following a financial disaster, that I had no hope that I would ever rebound. A friend of mine who is a successful lawyer didn't see it that way. He told me that I had just suffered a temporary set back and that, because I had a good education and had already tasted success, I would eventually "get on my horse again." He was right and not too long ago I personally thanked David Chavez for his comment that, unbeknownst to him, meant so much to me.

There was a point in my life when I realized that I could not run away any more. I did not feel that there was any place to go. I knew that I needed to make a stand. I rationalized that I had made a lot of mistakes but, after all, I was merely a human. I grew to believe that I had one last chance in life, and if I was going to be successful, I had to start over and perhaps repent. I felt guilty about the way I treated people as I had made so many unwise decisions that affected others. I made decisions many times for selfish reasons and other times out of fear, regret, or uncertainty. It was almost as if wisdom had slowly abandoned me.

Where Does It Hurt

Written by Noé Lara
May 10, 2007

Where does it hurt,
When you can't smile anymore.
Where does it hurt,
When your life is one big bore.

Where does it hurt,
When you feel your life is in vain.
Where does it hurt,
When all you feel is pain.

Where does it hurt,
When you are no longer free.
Where does it hurt,
When clouds define your destiny.

Where does it hurt,
when loved one's come and go.
Where does it hurt,
When your feeling oh so low.

Where does it hurt,
when in vain you try to sleep.
Where does it hurt,
When bad seeds you begin to reap.

My soul was broken and at night and alone, I felt contrite and cried bitter tears. This period lasted for several months, although it seemed like years. I didn't attend church, so I would give communion to myself. I drew strength from my family's religious background and would get some wine and a cracker and would take the Holy Supper. Continuing this practice for several months, I began to sense that God was near. I missed my children, and I felt that they needed me. I also was afraid that I had lost them and that I would never be able to show them the very best that I had. I was afraid that I would never get to experience all of their triumphs or to be there for them during their personal dark days. But what did I expect? I spent very little time with them when the family was together.

I was now on a journey, and I could sense the light at the end of the tunnel. It was almost as if I had walked all my life, and now I would be able to run and perhaps fly. I had a strong urge to win back yesterday's confidence, to strengthen my faith, and to begin believing in miracles again. I began to gain some balance in my life.

While in high school, I always strived for perfection. When I couldn't quite grasp a subject or thought, I had to rationalize that at a later time I would. However, I wanted to learn clearly and wanted to retain all of the information provided to me at the time. Since then I have learned that knowledge gained is never perfect, like mathematics. I also learned that human beings are not infallible. It is important to grasp the process of learning and to feel totally comfortable with what you learn in life. Sometimes it's a liberating feeling knowing that you don't know, nor will you ever know, everything. It's important to remember that some are called to be good musicians and others to be good scientists. It is okay not to be able to master both. I have accepted what the well known writer and psychiatrist Elizabeth Kubler-Ross was quoted as saying: "I am not OK and you are not OK, but…that's, OK."

Another gem that I have learned over the last 74 years is that life is not always what it seems. When I was growing up, I compared my parents' Mexican immigrant way of life to that of one lived in an Anglo culture, and I always found the old ways deficient and backward. The socialization that I was getting, and many times my own people would tell me that the Anglo way was superior. In my personal growth, I began to understand that we were not so different one from the other. I naively believed that once you obtained an education and accumulated wealth, you would be happy. I learned that this was a myth.

Problems of depression and lack of moral fiber also contribute immensely to one's character and, thus, success. My father had neither education nor money, but he was blessed with moral fiber and sound character. He was more of a hero than any successful businessman who arrived at his good fortune at the expense of good people. I just regret that it took me so long to learn this lesson. In my attempt to get ahead and to be accepted by the majority community, I did not value my parents' culture to the extent that I should have.

I struggled to find success in a world that many times seemed absurd. You are not supposed to take your life when it seems that you have everything going your way, especially when there are so many people struggling to just obtain a fraction of what you have. You are not supposed to die at a very young age when you haven't even gotten a chance to make your mark in the world. Thousands of young men, and innocent children and families, don't need to die because politicians want to flex their muscle or because careless or addicted people continue to drive recklessly. Hate towards other races, ethnic groups, and people of a different gender shouldn't exist if we are teaching in our spiritual sanctuaries that we are to love one another. In my opinion, educational, political, and religious institutions will not thrive, or perhaps even survive, if they exclude those who genuinely want to be included.

CHAPTER 17

How do you Spell Success?

The *Revised and Updated Oxford Dictionary* defines success as "the attainment of wealth, fame and position." The questions that I struggled with are: How much money does it take to be considered wealthy? What do you have to achieve to be called famous? How important must a job be to be able to call it a "position"?

Another definition from the same source is "the attainment of a goal." One sets many goals as we go through life. Because I saw the futility of a dead-end job as a farm laborer, I set as my immediate goal the attainment of a high school diploma. Achieving this, and feeling that this was not enough to be successful, I aimed at getting a college degree. I wanted a college degree so I could get a better job and thus appreciate a decent salary. In essence I wanted to get out of poverty, participate in the mainstream of society, and achieve the American Dream.

I also had the notion that having a college education would bring me respect, especially from the Anglo community. I was tired of the way Latinos were treated because they were uneducated and brown. Later in life I discovered that there were more than those two reasons for the way we were treated.

I knew that I wanted to have the opportunity to make money but at the beginning, I really never thought of making an enormous amount of money. I did, however, want to enjoy the finer things in life such as a nice home and a beautiful car and maybe go on a nice vacation once in a while. In terms of fame, I guess I never saw myself as ever being famous. I just do not have the personality for that. I did, however, want to some day leave a legacy. What that would look like, I had no idea.

Since then, I have grown tremendously, developing a sense of appreciation for the little things in life. To be able to find a good woman to grow old with. To accumulate a little money so it was possible to retire and perhaps have the opportunity, as Maslow described, to fulfill whatever potential I have.

Abraham Maslow developed a theory that stresses a hierarchy of needs. He stated that a lower need would have to be satisfied before the next need on the hierarchy could be approached. He identified these needs as physiological, safety, love and belonging, self-esteem, and self-actualization. Besides the fulfillment of one's potential, other qualities embodied by the self-actualized person are spontaneity, the ability to be in touch with one's feelings, high self-worth, and the development of one's own sense of spirituality. I am not sure whether anyone really ever achieves being self-actualized. However, it is comfortable to know that at least at this time, the first four rungs on the hierarchal ladder have been achieved.

Some years ago, I was fond of watching a television sitcom called *The Jeffersons*. The story line was that an African-American man had started a laundry business that eventually grew to the point where he owned a chain of laundries. One day he and his wife Louise were looking for a maid and advertised for one in the local paper. The scene is that of an African American woman coming to the door of their exclusive apartment to inquire about the job. Mr. Jefferson answers the door. She tells him, "I am sorry. I have the wrong door. I was looking for the Jeffersons." He responded that he was Mr. Jefferson. Her reaction was, "You mean we overcame and nobody told me?" She was referring to Dr. Martin Luther King Jr's civil rights campaign for inclusion and the song that inspired his followers, "We Shall Overcome".

I Am Not Like That Anymore

Written by Noé Lara
April 14, 2007

I fell and found myself in Hell,
I am not like that anymore

I have sipped wine from the cup of swine,
I am not like that anymore.

I sold my soul for a pot of gold,
I am not like that anymore.

I strayed far away intending to stay,
I am not like that anymore.

I left my pride on the other side,
I am not like that anymore.

I left my disease and found my peace,
I am not like that anymore.

I searched and I've found the most profound,
I am not like that anymore.

I traded my vice for my father's advice,
I am not like that anymore.

I now seek the wine of the divine,
I am not like that anymore.

God called my name so I am not the same,
I am not like that anymore.

Like the Jefferson's maid, I was always disappointed that when things happened that could be defined as success, I missed them. For example, I missed the feeling that I thought I was supposed to get when I graduated from college. I missed the emotional rush that people told me I would have. It was difficult feeling successful as a social worker because many times we could not measure the extent of our success. It isn't like being a successful architect who can take you to his buildings or show you the type of buildings or houses that he has designed for his clients. As a social worker, sometimes it is years before you can know whether what you said or tried to teach really made a difference in a client's life.

It has been my experience that success is better defined by others. I guess I never saw myself as being very successful. Yes, I accomplished several goals and perhaps, and in some circles, I obtained some recognition. However, I never saw myself doing anything unique. In fact, I often felt embarrassed when I received accolades. I felt that others were more deserving or that I was just doing my job. Many times, I felt that I was just plain lucky.

Growing up, I did not find it easy living in West Texas. My only models were my family and the Latino friends that my family had. There were no Latino educators, police officers, or elected officials, and there were few businessmen. As I became an adult, my perception of life was formed as I survived in the world of the Anglo and struggled to assimilate in their not-so-friendly dominant culture. My adult life began in West Texas, which at that time was not known for providing a friendly atmosphere to those not belonging to the majority community.

In my earlier years, and while working in the cotton fields, I was provided ample opportunity to daydream and to process feelings associated with the struggle to blend into the Anglo culture while feeling guilty for attempting to abandon my Mexican roots. I would daydream about being successful working at a job that would afford me the opportunity to help people. Still, I struggled with my insecure feelings that I could not compete against the majority who were Anglo. Not only the socialization provided in school, but my own family and Mexican culture seemed to impress upon me that what was Anglo was not only good, but superior. For example, when a white complexioned Latino child was born, people would say, "How pretty. He/she looks like a *bolillo* (Anglo)."

During my elementary years, other kids made fun of me for eating Mexican food, so my mother attempted to cut our tortillas into squares to make them look like bread. In the West Texas schools, we were punished for speaking in Spanish. The adult educators would tell us that it was for our own good to learn English as quickly as possible so we could be successful in school. But I sensed that many times they objected to our talking in Spanish because they felt that we were talking about them. Also, the teachers communicated to me that, somehow, my language was inferior.

On television, the Walt Disney Davy Crockett series also made it a little confusing for young Mexican-Americans. In the last scene of the Alamo segment, we saw Davy Crocket killing all of these mean Mexicans who didn't even seem to know how to fight.

And of course, there was the *Frito Bandido*. This gun–toting cartoon character projected a negative image of a Latino. The Frito Company thought this was an amusing way to sell their product. It wasn't hard for a young person to believe that everything associated with being Mexican was bad!

I gained a great deal of knowledge and wisdom from my work opportunities. I always enjoyed the social worker jobs. My training helped me attain some success in helping families turn their lives around. In my personal life, however, I made many foolish mistakes. I had opportunities to learn valuable lessons, but many times I chose not to.

Bullet

Written by Noé Lara
May 15, 2007

In my dream I was a bullet,
In a brown paper bag.
I sensed that I had power,
I guess I shouldn't brag.

I flew over highways,
At a tremendous speed.
I couldn't contain my emotions,
A little scared, yes indeed.

I guess some day I'll understand,
This dream I had one day.
Flying all over the country,
Because I couldn't stay.

I don't know why I didn't walk,
or why I didn't run.
I just flew like there was no tomorrow,
Although not having too much fun.

Inside a paper bag,
No holes for me to see.
But I could smell the hot tar highway,
Pushing me, pushing me.

Now that I am no longer young,
I don't dream this anymore.
I sense I'm still a bullet,
But I finally found the door.

I opened it so carefully,
To see what I had missed.
I saw some wondrous things,
On the bag I made a list.

I saw mountains, I saw rivers.
I saw trees and a bright blue sky.
I laid a blanket under a tree,
And there my dream and I did lie.

I made decisions that caused my loved ones and me a great deal of pain. I was aware that I was making foolish choices, but I did not have the self-discipline to not make them. It seemed that my desire to accumulate wealth and become respected fanned the flames of ambition and false pride. I used my insecurities to compensate for the fact that I was not well grounded for success.

In education, I finished high school and earned a Bachelor and Masters degree. Throughout the years I have held licenses in real estate, construction, insurance, securities, and in social work. You might say that I have achieved success in the area of education. If money is one of the measuring sticks for success, I have made decent money working in these areas. However, I have also lost a lot of money because I rationalized that it takes money to make money. Unwise investments and foolish pride led me down a path of financial set-backs. I had a habit of putting the cart before the horse, and I would spend more money then I made.

As young adults, we members of the Baby Boomer generation were not known for reflecting on the present. Instead, we talked about the big picture and sacrificed our families for the "greater good" that was to be found in the future. In my case I feel that I never appreciated the opportunities presented to me. At least, I did not appreciate them to the level that I should have. It wasn't until recently that I began to learn to save money and not spend so much unwisely. I owe much of this to my wife Diana, who is very conservative when it comes to spending money without a good plan.

I do believe however, that to be successful is to enjoy a good relationship with your family and to earn their respect, if not their admiration. As of this moment, I do not have this with my son and am growing less confident that I ever will. In this area, I admit that I have not succeeded.

I really never expected to make as much money as I was making when I retired, but the opportunities that presented themselves helped me to get over my financial set-back. In this respect, education and the social work field were very good to me. I enjoyed the work while enjoying a decent income and appreciating an adequate retirement plan.

Overall, I would rate myself as having achieved a great deal of success but not in the way that we normally think of success. I had the discipline to earn a Bachelor of Arts and a Masters degree in Sociology. I always admire young people who get through college, as many quit school and others never even attend. There were many times when I wanted to give up, but I hung in there, as there were many people who were counting on me. No matter what anybody says, college is not easy. It is especially not easy for minority students who have no family role models to guide and inspire them. However, it's important to remember that for the majority of people, it is doable.

I remember that when my son Noé graduated from High School, we argued because he wanted to go to an art school in the state of Colorado. I wanted him to go to the University of New Mexico or to Texas Tech University, my alma mater. It suddenly dawned on me that I was not having the argument that many parents were having with their kids about just staying in school. I then told my son that he could attend whatever college that he wanted to, and that I would help him. I had been an example of one who had gone to college, so there was no doubt in his mind that he was going to college. The only question was where? This was a good feeling for me.

I also believe that my daughter Elizabeth Ann got a college degree because her mother and I served as examples in that we both have college degrees.

I believe that I was also successful in that I tried things. For example, it was a big deal for a little Mexican-American farm boy to decide to accept a job in Washington, D.C., some 1,200 miles from my hometown. This was unknown territory, and I did not have a clue before leaving for the District if I could make it in the big city. I was scared to death! However, I not only made it, but I excelled to the point that I was later promoted to even higher responsibilities within the agency.

As a result of my work with the Housing Assistance Council (HAC), I was tapped by Governor Bruce King to direct the New Mexico State Housing Authority. This also carried with it an awesome responsibility, and at first I was not sure whether I was up for the challenge. But I stayed with the governor for four years and went on to work for the incoming governor for another six months.

Also, I managed to study and earn licenses which permitted me to try to make it in business. Although I was not very successful in business, I did take a risk. I took a risk in the home construction and in the housing development ventures that I launched. For a while, I was also sold life insurance plans and securities. I rehabilitated and built houses while I successfully packaged multi-family rental complexes. These apartments are still serving low and moderate-income families in rural New Mexico.

I attempted things long enough for me to discover what I did and did not enjoy doing. I wasn't going to be like those who are now old men but still talk about the opportunities they had, but who always found an excuse for not taking advantage of them. You can't succeed unless you attempt things.

I now find myself doing things that were only blurred dreams prior to retirement. Although not yet a master, I am becoming a pretty decent artist. I am finding out that many people like my oil paintings almost as much as I like painting them. I have also rekindled my love for poetry. I am writing poems to go along with my paintings, and many people have found them stimulating and thought-provoking and encouraged me to publish them. I published them in a book titled, *El Mundo de Noé*, (Noé's World)

I always wondered whether anyone besides my family and close friends would be interested in my story. I have found so much joy in recollecting my experiences and once again feeling those emotions that sparked fire in my soul when they were happening. It has also been fun communicating with my brothers and sisters and comparing notes for accuracy and perspective. I have discovered that we sometimes view life experiences using a different set of lenses. Nonetheless, all of my family is very happy that I decided to write this book, and they are very proud of me for my effort.

I am now confident that I have reached that "aha" moment in my life. I am beginning to get it! I believe that I have had unique opportunities that perhaps have not been available to the average person. I also am proud of myself for learning to pick my battles and not waste time on insignificant disagreements that just drain your energies but do nothing to move you forward in life.

Life has been one "hell of a ride", and I have not come out of it unscathed. I have, however, grown more appreciative of those who enjoy the gift of patience. I have slowed my pace and have found pleasure in taking the time to appreciate the people around me and the many gifts and blessings that I have enjoyed.

I will not dwell on my mistakes or blame others because things did not turn out the way I had earlier hoped they would. I have gained a deep trust in the Universe and accept that the way my life turned out perhaps followed a better plan.

In my Garden I am Free

Written by Noé Lara
April 21, 2007

I was born a slave.
A slave of man, a slave of thoughts,
a slave of words, a slave of doubts.

I am slave no more.
I found the answer, I found the key,
I opened the door,
And I found me.

I no longer have to fear,
I quit searching, because I found,
The most obvious secret,
and the most profound.

I found the secret.
I won the prize,
It wasn't hidden,
It was in plain site.

In my garden I'm happy,
In my garden I'm free.
I don't have to impress anybody,
it's me and only me.

I don't need a license,
I don't need a degree.
I am happy growing flowers,
for the whole world to see.

I will share my good fortune,
My friends and my dreams.
Just like I share my roses,
I'll share the beautiful things I've seen.

Daughter Nella

A painting of the Lara farm house by Noe Lara

Grandfather Noe With Grandson Liam At Old Town, Albuquerque

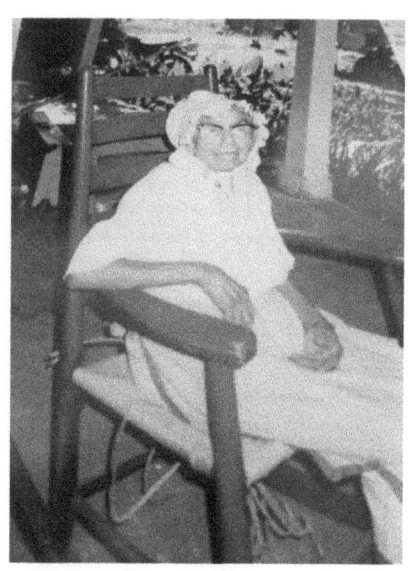

My Mother On Porch At Lara Farm House In Lubbock

Noe And Diana With Grandchildren

¿CUÁNTAS PÍSCAS?

Noe At Balloon Fiesta In Albuquerque

Noe At Tome Hill In Nm Pilgrimate Site

Painting of Cotton Trailer and Scale

¿CUÁNTAS PÍSCAS?

Noe and son Noe Domingo

ABOUT THE AUTHOR

Noé Lara was born on a ranch located 20 miles from Austin, the capitol of the state of Texas. He was one of 13 children born to Mexican immigrants don David and doña Lola Lara. The Lara family spent 10 years in the migrant stream which took them from East Texas as far north as Wisconsin. They then settled in West Texas where cotton crops were abundant and seasonal work provided a living for large families willing to work.

Noé attended Texas Tech University in Lubbock, Texas and earned both a Bachelor and a Masters degree in Sociology. He started his social work career in Lubbock, Texas but moved to Washington D.C. where he worked for a national housing corporation dedicated to rural housing issues. He moved to New Mexico in 1973. He became the Regional director of the Housing Assistance Council. In 1980, he was recruited by Governor Bruce King to be the State Housing Authority director. He and his wife Diana now call Los Lunas, New Mexico home.

In November 2005, Noé retired from a social work career working for the State of New Mexico. However, he continued to work as an adjunct professor at the University of New Mexico, Valencia Campus (UNM-VC). He retired from UNM-VC in 2015. Noé has always been a student of people and institutions, a reason that he became a sociology professor.

Noé is an artist, a musician, and a poet. He derives much inspiration from his past and present work experiences, from his rich Mexican culture, and from his family life experiences living in rural New Mexico.

www.ingramcontent.com/pod-product-compliance
Ingram Content Group UK Ltd.
Pitfield, Milton Keynes, MK11 3LW, UK
UKHW022227230426
12048UKWH00016BA/1108